"This book is not just for Americans. Not just for patriots. Not just for pacifists. Not just for Christians. This is a book for everyone who would dare to listen to those who return from war and ask not for honor but for permission to be honest. This is for everyone who longs to rediscover our humanity, and Jesus' message, in a world at war."

Jarrod McKenna, Australian Peace Award recipient and World Vision advisor

"This is an unsettling book (in all the right ways), written by a pioneer for peace who knows what conflict is like 'on the ground.' Music is woven into the story, but the profounder music is that of Christ's shalom."

Jeremy Begbie, Duke University

"Logan Mehl-Laituri articulates how God laid claim to his life as he wrestled in the dark valley of moral ambiguity, the dialogue of contrary forces tugging for control of his life. He is a person of courage, of heroic valor, who sees his duty and does it; he is a child of God, since he was reborn on the fourth of July."

Herman Keizer Jr., U.S. Army (retired), and director of chaplains, emeritus, Christian Reformed Church of North America

The Challenge of Faith,
Patriotism & Conscience

Logan Mehl-Laituri

Foreword by Shane Claiborne

IVP Books

An imprint of InterVarsity Press
Downers Grove, Illinois

InterVarsity Press
P.O. Box 1400, Downers Grove, IL 60515-1426
World Wide Web: www.ivpress.com
E-mail: email@ivpress.com

InterVarsity Press® is the book-publishing division of InterVarsity Christian Fellowship/USA®, a movement of students and faculty active on campus at hundreds of universities, colleges and schools of nursing in the United States of America, and a member movement of the International Fellowship of Evangelical Students. For information about local and regional activities, write Public Relations Dept., InterVarsity Christian Fellowship/USA, 6400 Schroeder Rd., P.O. Box 7895, Madison, WI 53707-7895, or visit the IVCF website at <www.intervarsity.org>.

All Scripture quotations, unless otherwise indicated, are taken from the THE HOLY BIBLE, NEW INTERNATIONAL VERSION®, NIV® Copyright © 1973, 1978, 1984, 2011 by Biblica, Inc.™ Used by permission. All rights reserved worldwide.

While all stories in this book are true, some names and identifying information in this book have been changed to protect the privacy of the individuals involved.

Cover design: Cindy Kiple
Interior design: Beth Hagenberg
Images: dog tag: © John Clines/iStockphoto
         American flag: © Derek Audette/iStockphoto

ISBN 978-0-8308-3652-9

Printed in the United States of America ∞

Library of Congress Cataloging-in-Publication Data

Mehl-Laituri, Logan, 1981-
Reborn on the fourth of July: The challenge of faith, patriotism & conscience / Logan Mehl-Laituri.
     p. cm.
   Includes bibliographical references.
   ISBN 978-0-8308-3652-9 (pbk.: alk. paper)
   1. Soldiers—Religious life. 2. Conscientious objection. 3. Military ethics. 4. Peace—Religious aspects—Christianity. 5. Mehl-Laituri, Logan, 1981 - I. Title.
   BV4588.M44 2012
   261.8'73092—dc23
                                                                    2012009663

P   18   17   16   15   14   13   12   11   10   9   8   7   6   5   4   3   2   1
Y   27   26   25   24   23   22   21   20   19   18   17   16   15   14   13   12

For Daniel and Katie, each of whom pressed me to a deeper knowledge of the beauty of life through the tragedy of death, and in doing so moved me to a greater appreciation for everything in between

Contents

Foreword

✭

I REMEMBER THE FIRST TIME I heard about him, a decorated U.S. Army Veteran from the 1991 Gulf War. I remember reading the letters he wrote home from the war, where he told his family how hard it was to kill. He told them he felt like he was turning from a human being into an animal because day after day it became a little easier to kill. He went on to do one of the worst acts of domestic terrorism the United States has ever seen: the Oklahoma City bombing in 1995. His name was Timothy McVeigh.

Timothy came home from the Gulf War horrified, crazy, dehumanized . . . the worst domestic terrorist the United States has ever seen. His essays cry out against the bloodshed he saw and created in Iraq. He wrote (in his "Essay on Hypocrisy"), "Do people think that government workers in Iraq are any less human than those in Oklahoma City? Do they think that Iraqis don't have families who will grieve and mourn the loss of their loved ones? Do people believe that the killing of foreigners is somehow different than the killing of Americans?" No doubt his mind had been tragically deranged by what he saw and what he did. He bombed Oklahoma City in hopes that complacent Americans could see what "collateral damage" looks like, and cry out against the bloodshed everywhere, even in Iraq. Instead, the government that had trained him to kill killed him, to teach the rest of us that it is wrong to kill. Timothy McVeigh lost his mind in a war.

★ ★ ★

I remember hearing about another Army vet from the Iraq War, whose letters sent tears rolling down my cheeks. He was a forward observer in the U.S. Army, a position that meant he was literally "on the front lines," observing all the casualties on the battlefield. After five years in the military, he felt a collision in his soul, not unlike the one felt by Timothy McVeigh. His name is Logan Mehl-Laituri. And his story ends very different from Timothy's. Logan has done something beautiful instead of something terrible with his pain. Because of what he has seen and experienced, he has quickly become one of the most innovative and credible voices for peace in the Western Hemisphere.

I will never forget the first letters I got from Logan as he wrestled with how to serve both God and country as a U.S. soldier. He described it as feeling like he was trying to serve two masters, and he confessed that he didn't feel like he could carry a cross and a sword at the same time.

What's exceptional about Logan is that his commitment to peace did not come from reading a bunch of books or watching indie films. He's not a granola-eating, long-haired hippie (not that I'm dissing granola-eating, long-haired hippies). Logan's heart for peace comes from simply reading the Bible and wanting to follow Jesus. His nonviolence comes from seeing the cost of war and how different it looks from the gospel of Jesus. It's hard to argue with someone who hates war because they've lived war.

I know that, like me, you will find Logan's ideas fresh, nuanced and challenging. He's dangerous because he's got some serious street cred. But there is also an innocence in his words and witness, like that of a child I remember in my neighborhood here in Philadelphia who asked why people carry guns in the city when there aren't that many deer to hunt. Logan is refreshing because he doesn't fit into any box, label or category—it's part of his charm. When you think you've figured him out he will say something stunningly wise and remarkably different from what you thought was coming. I recall hearing someone begin to accuse Logan of being anti-American; he quickly said, "I love America. I just love God more." Logan has taught me that God loves America, but God's love doesn't stop at any borders. Our Bible does not say that "God so loved America" but that "God so loved the world."

When Logan decided that he could not kill anyone because he is a Christian, you'd think he would just leave the military. But instead, in order to honor his commitment and service, he said, "I'm glad to stay, and even go back to Iraq. I just can't carry a gun or hurt anyone." And it is this kind of logic that got him discharged with an "adjustment disorder." When that happened I remember telling Logan, "You may be crazy. But you are not alone." Indeed, as Logan will tell you in this book, he is not alone at all. There are "soldier saints" throughout history who have decided, as Logan did, "For Christ I can die, but I cannot kill."

The first time I went to Iraq as a Christian peacemaker in 2003, where I lived in Baghdad during the bombing, Logan might have been on the other side of the bombs and guns. I saw the insanity of war as I worked in hospitals and held kids whose bodies were riddled with missile fragments. I saw that "collateral damage." But what Logan has taught me is that the innocent victims in Iraq and Afghanistan are not the only collateral damage. There is another collateral damage from war: our own children, our own mothers and fathers in the U.S. military. As I have walked with Logan over the past five years, we have letter after letter from U.S. soldiers who have felt the same collision in their souls that Logan felt. We have heard young kids who grew up in poverty talk about the "economic draft," explaining that they only went into the military in order to try and go to college. They had never wanted to have to kill anyone. Logan has taught me about this other collateral damage. He knows folks who have died in war, but he also knows folks who have died from war—folks who have come home and hung themselves. We live in an age where more soldiers are dying from suicide than are dying in combat. We have seen young men and women over and over feeling war kill the good in them. And Logan has said *"Enough!"*

Author Henri Nouwen coined a brilliant image as he spoke of "the wounded healer." Nouwen points out that our wounds are not something we should be embarrassed about; they are the very things that can give us the power to heal others. Our wounds are not a liability; they are our credibility. It's not our degrees and titles but our wounds that empower us to help others. The best folks to help women in domestic violence are women who have survived domestic violence. The best folks to help heroin addicts in their recovery are folks who are recovering themselves. And some of the most credible voices for peace are folks who have seen the horrors of war. Logan's wounds are his credentials, and he is now spending his life helping other soldiers who have similar battle scars and who have felt the same collision between serving God and country.

When Logan talks about supporting our troops, he has something different in mind than simply sending them off to war again and bringing them home and trying to help them recover from the horrible things they have seen and done. He is done with the "pick up the sword, die by the sword" thing. We have learned that lesson all too well. Like Jesus, Logan knows there is another way.

★ ★ ★

One of my favorite prophetic images in the Bible is found in Isaiah 2 and Micah 4, which alike speak of God's people beating their swords into plows: "They will beat their swords into plowshares and their spears into pruning hooks. . . . Nation will not take up sword against nation, nor will they train for war anymore." It's this wonderful image of transforming the things that have brought death into things that bring life. But as you read it closely you will notice something. The prophets are very clear that peace does not begin with "the nations" but with "the people."

The people begin to beat their own swords into farm tools, their own spears into pruning hooks. It is the people, perhaps even the soldiers themselves, who lead the way. It is not the kings and presidents who lead us to peace (in fact, they keep leading us into wars), but it is the people of God who refuse to continue to carry those weapons and fight in those wars. Only then do the prophets say that "nation will not rise up against nation, nor will they train for war anymore."

Isaiah goes on to write, "The people walking in darkness have seen a great light" (Isaiah 9:2), and then, "Every warrior's boot used in battle and every garment rolled in blood will be destined for burning, will be fuel for the fire" (Isaiah 9:5). Logan Mehl-Laituri is one of the contemporary prophets for peace, denouncing the evils of war and pronouncing the nonviolent love of Jesus. Listen closely, dear friends, and be encouraged; there are many Logans out there.

Shane Claiborne

A Note to the Reader

☆

SOME DISCLAIMERS ARE IN order before you start reading . . .

A *Soldier* is a member of the United States Army, but *soldier* is a word that describes members of armed forces throughout history. Where I have capitalized the word, I am describing a member of the United States Army (including the Reserves and National Guard). Where *soldier* appears in the middle of a sentence and I do not capitalize it, I am using the term generically to describe members of military forces anywhere, any time. If I reference members of other branches of the United Stated Armed Forces, I will capitalize their titles (e.g., Marines, Sailors, Airmen).

In most military units, the acronym *CO* stands for "Commanding Officer." Here, however, since conscientious objection is a focus of discussion (and the first word is likely to tongue tie many readers), *CO* will always stand for "conscientious objector."

It is important to note that my military service was conducted almost exclusively in the company of men. I went to one of the last Basic Training battalions to train only male recruits (Ft. Sill, Oklahoma). Once I got into my advanced training in field artillery, my specialty was characterized as combat arms, which remains (at the date of publication) closed to women. I rarely reference women in the military because that was my experience; it should not be taken as reflective of the military as a whole.

The use of masculine pronouns in reference to God is a highly contentious issue for many people. Where I could not use gender-neutral language, I have opted to use masculine imagery, though I recognize doing so is at best inadequate and at worst inaccurate. God is not a man, nor is God a woman; I have as much issue with referring to God as "he" as I do referring to God as "she," but in the absence of consensus, I have opted to go with what is likely familiar to the most readers. This is, however, an important subject that I hope will continue to be explored by the church, laypeople and leadership alike.

I use music rather generously in the text, weaving lyrics into narrative. Where I have done so, I've cited the band, song title, album, record and year released (in that order) in the notes section. I do not want to take any form of credit for the music in this way; I have opted for stylistic fluidity as a way of articulating how music became a part of my life. For me there is little separating music from monologue. I think music, particularly hymns (including contemporary Christian musicians and their craft), could stand to be much more fully incorporated into Christian life. Creeds and hymns were ways in which early Christian communities learned the faith, and churches would do well to consider how "Christian music" should be brought under closer consideration for what and how it speaks to congregations.

Finally, there is a lot to be said about the justice of the particular war in which I fought, but I won't say it here. Not just because I fail to agree with the theology of *any* organized violence, but because this is not a book about war; it is a book about God.

Introduction

☆

IN THE LAST INTERVIEW HE recorded before his death, Jewish theologian Rabbi Abraham Heschel insisted

> that there is a meaning beyond absurdity . . . that every little deed
> counts, that every word has power, and that we do, everyone,
> our share to redeem the world, in spite of all absurdities, and
> all the frustrations, and all the disappointment. And above all,
> remember that the meaning of life is to live life as if it were a
> work of art.[1]

When I read this in 2007, I wept. After surviving combat, all was absurd; everything had lost meaning. Life was not worth living. It took some years before I got to the point at which I could believe words like Heschel's, before I could believe that my life could be a work of art.

When I first came home, I listened to a lot of music by Jack Johnson. Had I listened to heavy metal or something, I may have killed myself; so much aimless frustration only makes Post-Traumatic Stress Disorder (PTSD) worse, especially at high volume. Some music rages, but some of it mourns. Music became a kind of order to my chaos. It's why I did not segment this book into chapters;

in music a movement separates distinct sections of a larger piece, separated by silence. Don't read this book in one sitting; let *it* sit with *you*, in silence when necessary.

You might find that this book has a confessional nature; there are a number of very personal details, some of which are quite grotesque, details I think the American church should learn how to receive. I believe very strongly that confession is a lost art that the church must recover not only to reintegrate its many thousands of soldiers but to narrate our story honestly—our hands are not clean. In a way, this book is a series of confessions (though that title was taken already) specific to one soldier, but perhaps representative of a great many.

The first time I thought about writing about my experiences, it was because I was angry about the plight of fellow veterans and service members. When I learned that seventeen veterans were taking their own lives every day and nobody was talking about it—not even the military community—I got incredibly angry. Luckily, I had a community that surrounded me with love and did not allow anger to have the last word. I spent a lot of time in my prayer closet (which, in retrospect, should have been fitted for soundproofing). I also chopped a lot of firewood in those days.

Anger is good at leading us out of the pews and into the streets, bullhorn in hand, fist in the air. But done poorly, even "Christian" protests can be self-gratuitous and shortsighted. Yelling at the subject of our anger can feel good for a time, but the feeling fades fast and is usually replaced by more anger. If our prophetic action is not matched equally by prophetic piety, our amplified outbursts are nothing but resounding gongs or clanging symbols.

I've seen Christians assume that anger fueled by grief and pain has no positive value at all. Such anger is passively overlooked or actively dismissed. That there are so few liturgies of lament for the longest war in American history worries me tremendously. It seems to me that the degree to which people embrace suffering is proportional to the degree to which they can experience joy. We worship *because* we've seen exactly how wretched this world can be, how deeply we need Jesus, because we can see exactly how amazing is his grace. Evil is not passing away; it's here to stay, and it calls us to action.

My anger never went away; it simply transformed into something more practical. I began recording my memories, at first for counselors at the Veterans Administration but eventually for myself. Every word had power. My conscience *burned*; God moved in my fingers as they would peck out story after story, some published, some private. And yet the subject of those stories, I found, was not me but God.

Heschel said that a religious person "holds God and [humankind] in one thought at one time, at all times, who suffers harm done to others, whose greatest passion is compassion, whose greatest strength is love and defiance of despair."[2] When I read most nonfiction, I scribble notes to myself in the margins. When I read Heschel, I write notes to God. If this is a book about a religious person, and I hope that it is, then it is as much about God as it is about me.

This is a book about what God did in the life of one soldier and what might be possible for and in the lives of others (in the military or not). It is more than an altar call; it is a rallying cry. If you are like me, if you have followed Jesus all the way to the gates of hell and now can't rid yourself of the sights and smells, despair not. All is not lost: you are not alone. You were *never* alone.

Make no mistake, I am still angry. A lot of what I have accomplished has been fueled by the deep sense of betrayal and despair I have felt in the last decade. But our anger must be transformed by faith if we are to avoid being consumed. There at the intersection of righteous anger and patient faith, we find hope.

This testimony is an exercise in hope.

MOVEMENT ONE

"What a cruel thing is war . . . to fill our hearts with hatred instead of love for our neighbors, and to devastate the fair face of this beautiful world."
ROBERT E. LEE, COMMANDING GENERAL,
CONFEDERATE STATES OF AMERICA

"The truth belongs to God, the mistakes were mine."
MEWITHOUTYOU, CONTEMPORARY CHRISTIAN-AMERICAN MUSICIANS

"God, have mercy on me, a sinner!"
PENITENT JEWISH-ROMAN PUBLIC SERVANT (LUKE 18)

Ambushed by
My Capacity to Kill

★

"THAT GUN STILL WORKING? Light those cars up, light 'em up!"

The next thing I sensed after Sergeant Harris's muffled yell was a piece of lightning making contact with my neck, tumbling down the skin of my back, having slipped inside the plate of my bulletproof vest. The loose brass tumbled electrically down my spine. Specialist Baker, our .50 cal gunner, had let loose, turning the exteriors of a few white trucks into dimpled golf balls.

More spent brass casings rained down around me as I radioed the command vehicle to report that we had made contact. By our sixth month in Iraq, our ears had become accustomed to the roar of gunfire, and I had adapted my radio procedure accordingly, keying the handmike only in between loud bursts of semi and automatic weapons and trying my best to listen during the brief moments of relative silence in between.

Just a few minutes before the ambush, I had commented ominously that I had "a bad feeling" about our circumstances. It sounded like a bad movie, so cliché it almost hurt to say it out loud. It was June

22, 2004, and my infantry platoon was in Najaf, providing security for a long convoy of heavy tactical trucks—many more than our nine up-armored Humvees could reasonably protect. An explosion had rocked an intersection as my vehicle passed through. No one was injured, but we stopped in order to secure the intersection for the passing trucks. Without vehicular armor or heavy weapons mounted atop their cabs, many of our drivers were particularly vulnerable. I was positioned behind Sergeant Harris on the passenger side of the vehicle, away from the line of trucks. Specialist Daniels, our driver that day, joined Harris outside the vehicle in a heartbeat, their twin M-4s blazing.

I raised my weapon to prepare to return fire, but my priority was the radio, specifically raising the lieutenant who so far had failed to respond. My anger skyrocketed at the fact that we had been attacked and that the junior officer had failed to remain in touch at such a dire moment. My blood felt as though it was boiling, like a pot of water in the desert heat of that June day. When Daniels ducked back in the vehicle to correct his jammed weapon, I forced the radio into his hand, insisting abruptly that he continue to attempt to raise the lieutenant. With that, I threw my door open and moved my selector switch from "safe" to "semi" in the fluid movement I had rehearsed endlessly since arriving in Kuwait over six months earlier.

If our truck were an analog clock, Harris, near the hood of our vehicle, was scanning an area from roughly 12 to 4, and from his position at the turret sticking out of the roof of the vehicle, Baker could sweep from just about 6 to 1. Just as they had been trained in infantry Boot Camp, their fields of fire just overlapped. My field ended up being about 3 to 7, which also happened to be where the HEMTTs (Heavy Expanded Mobility Tactical Trucks) were rumbling by. Nonetheless, I scanned my lane for actionable targets—anyone with a weapon or something resembling a remote control.

We had heard small arms fire shortly before the explosion, so we were expecting resistance. With Baker on the .50 cal and Harris rampaging with his M-4, my heart raced with morbid anticipation. Left and right my eyes darted, eagerly searching for an excuse to fire my weapon. Down an alley, a small mass of people was scurrying for cover, trying to avoid the Americans and their guns. I lifted my rifle to eye level and peered at them through my Aimpoint sight. My attention rested on one man in particular, who kept peering back at us despite the danger. The rest of the crowd had tunnel vision looking for any alley or crevice that might serve as protection from stray bullets, but this guy kept looking over his shoulder. Was that a radio in his hand, or was he just biting his nails? My index finger dropped from the magazine well down onto the curved metal trigger of my M-4 as I considered the actionability of this particular target.

How had I gotten to this point?

Coming into the World
and Going to Church

✮

I HAD ALWAYS THOUGHT OF MYSELF as having a soft heart. My older sister reminded me recently that when we would fight as kids, truces between the two of us would last longer than they would between her and our brother because I was so "sweet and tender-hearted." Sensitivity to my surroundings, whether people or places, has always been a part of who I am.

I remember how I felt when my brother fell from a third story balcony when our zip line failed. He and I had built it together; I felt terrible. I could imagine the terror of falling, could almost feel the blinding crack of his forehead on the ground, his limbs thudding around his torso awkwardly. The most pain I've ever felt in my life was hearing his screams echo through the emergency room as the doctors broke his arm later that evening in order to reset it. The pain was so real I might as well have fallen myself.

My heart broke for my parents in different ways. They worked as teachers in some of the most economically depressed areas of Orange County, California. My mom would tell us about knives being brought to school, of sexual assaults and violent fights her sixth and seventh grade students would get into. My parents knew exactly how broken our public schools were, and they worked unenviably hard to put as many of their four children through private schools as possible. They got as far as sending me, their third, to safer, more prestigious schools up through the fifth grade, but it drove them to bankruptcy.

Attending private schools as a kid made me particularly attuned to our family's relative lack of wealth. I had no sense of affluence; I only knew that my friends would be picked up in BMWs and Lexuses while my mom would drive up in a beaten up, brown Dodge Caravan. To contribute in my own little way, I would go around the house turning off lights in the evenings. It was a token gesture of gratitude, perhaps, for having the inscrutable dignity to continue to pick us up every day.

My parents worked long hours, more than any other teacher I ever encountered, and generated little recognition for their work.[1] I watched them work for poor compensation in questionable conditions for no other reason than that they were passionate about it. They cared for their students in a way that exceeded my understanding. Teaching for my parents was a sign of their hope in the future their students could unlock; education pointed beyond GPAs and class schedules, steering some of those least likely to succeed in society nonetheless toward success.

As a child, I never would have used the term *sacramental* to describe education. I probably would have used the word *headache*. But there is something sacred about teaching and learning, something incalculably holy about the transmission of knowledge. The church speaks of sacraments as being signs, symbolic things or gestures of that which we can't quite yet grasp. The Greek word we translate from is *mysterion*, literally, "mystery."[2] Something in my parent's irrepressible devotion to teaching cultivated in me a profound and unexplainable respect not only for each of them, but also for the importance of education.

Not having had a "religious" upbringing allowed me to assign religious undertones to things, like education, that otherwise may not be popularly understood as religious. I hadn't been trained to see God only in those things formally characterized as sacraments. *Life* was sacrament. My grandma making me little peanut butter and jelly triangles at three in the morning when I couldn't sleep—that was sacrament. Ducks landing in our pool was sacrament. God was in all of it! Church was where you went to talk more deliberately about Jesus, but it was not always as spiritual as those other things that I found holy. In church I was bored, but in life I found joy.

✱ ✱ ✱

When I got old enough to understand a few things, I saw churchgoing as a kind of tactic, a game that I was supposed to learn how to play. There was a distinct language and culture around Christianity that did not follow me to school or back home. I remember thinking of it as a set of clothes; I wore it when it was appropriate and shed it when it was not. After all, since I wasn't doing anything wrong, like drugs or premarital sex, Christianity didn't seem to have much relevancy for my life.

On the other hand, I had no reason to think of myself as being anything but Christian. When I began attending a youth group, it hadn't even entered my mind to consider a temple or a mosque. Why would it have? I was American; that meant I was a Christian, right?

The church my family attended when I was young was a given; I didn't learn about why we attended until I was much older. A winter baby, I had contracted infantile bronchitis. The doctors worried I might not survive, so when a family friend encouraged my parents to allow her Episcopal priest to visit, they happily obliged. They might not have attributed my survival to God, but it made for a pretty good pitch to attend church. We went until I was about five years old, but I have only scattered memories of the parish.

As I began high school, I found my way to church once again. Or maybe church found its way to me. On December 27, two days after my fourteenth birthday, my parents announced that they would be separating.

I didn't see it coming. I was young and couldn't read the signs my older siblings noticed. Like any devastated kid in the midst of a split, I wanted attention. To get it, I started shoplifting. One day in February a plainclothes employee at a chain drugstore stopped me outside the sliding automatic doors and asked me if I planned on paying for the two candy bars I had in my pocket. I blathered something incoherent and defensive and I ended up in the store manager's office, where calls to my parents went unanswered until the manager had to close for the night. They had no choice but to call the police and have them pick me up. I watched, hands cuffed behind my back, as the officer opened the front door of his car to put something inside. I asked him if that was where I was going to be riding. "No," he replied. "The bad guys sit in the back."

The idea that I was a "bad guy" was driven home later when my mom came to pick me up at the station. I was mortified: she arrived with a face swollen by tears, entering without saying a word, not even looking at me. My mom had always been strong, but here I was seeing her broken. I knew that I had done something terribly wrong. She didn't punish me—she didn't have to. I had learned my lesson in a more visceral and memorable way than either of us bargained for.

Less than a week later, I began going to a local youth group. I figured it was what I was supposed to do when I did something wrong: go to church. I remember the worship music the most; the six or seven songs we sang at the beginning of the meetings were always my favorite part of the gatherings. Unlike the rest of the kids, I didn't stand any more than I had to, and I rarely clapped to the beat. Often, I would simply move to a dark corner of the youth sanctuary, close my eyes and sway to the rhythm, singing just loud enough to hear myself and to be heard by God.

People sometimes inadvertently cast introverts as being isolationists, but I knew I wasn't alone in those dark corners. It was simply where I was most comfortable. The youth group was made up of kids from my high school. I was not as wealthy as they were. Over time, the gatherings grew on me, and I came to appreciate them more with every passing year. Going to church on Wednesdays and Sundays made me feel more human; the social tensions eased slightly, and academic expectations were put on pause.

I remember very little about what I learned in youth group—or, more accurately, I can't remember where I learned the things I came to know about Jesus. Some of it had been there as long as I remember, seeds from that little church of my youth sprouting later in adolescence. For example, I knew that God knew everything; you couldn't lie to God. I also remember thinking about the more difficult passages in Scripture, like turning the other cheek and selling everything you own, and wondering why people didn't do them. I figured those passages were like the social games we played in school; perhaps there were different rules for different cliques.

In the mornings at school, we reminded ourselves, with our hands placed reverently over our hearts, that our nation stood indivisibly "under God." At Boy Scout meetings, we promised to do our duty to God and country alike. I made the rank of First Class Scout before I finally memorized the Lord's Prayer we would recite at the end of each meeting.

Being a Christian was part and parcel to being American. Or at least as far as I could tell it was. So when I began talking to an Army recruiter about enlisting, it was not merely a patriotic task; it had religious undertones. To defend the country was to serve God. It was not something I actively believed, but it was an assumption that I never questioned, and it became in some way true, whether I recognized it or not. My inquiry into the Army was more than a strictly practical choice—I was searching for meaning, looking to enter into a story that was bigger than I was. I would receive money for college, but the exchange was an act of faith: how would I know what lay between my enlistment and my discharge? I was gambling with my life, but at the time, the odds were good.

Going into the Army

★

MY CLOSEST FRIEND IN HIGH school had signed up for the Army Reserves as an ammunition specialist, and he invited me to a small demonstration at the Reserve Center. When a recruiter approached me, our conversation fell quickly to my need of college money. I scheduled an appointment with him later that week.

I had never felt particularly patriotic. I loved my country, but that was not a significant motivating factor for much of anything. I wanted to go to college, to honor my parents' sacrifice, but the financial toll was one I dared not ask my parents to endure. I knew up front exactly what I wanted from the recruiter: as much help with college as possible.

My parents joined me for a meeting with the commander of the recruiting station. My mom had tunnel vision for getting me into college; every question she asked was about the reliability of things like the Army College Fund and GI Bill. As it turns out, the Veterans Administration has an incredibly complex and inefficient process for veterans who are trying to get their monetary and medical benefits after discharge. There have been some gains in that regard in recent years, but—very much like combat—the picture painted for me at enlistment was much different than the reality I would come to experience.

I wanted to be stationed in Hawaii, but when I arrived at the military processing station in Los Angeles, the only slot they had in a coastal state was for North Carolina. I shrugged my approval, but I became slightly more animated when I was asked if I wanted to attend airborne training. I have an adventurous soul, and there are few things that could have piqued my interest more at that age than jumping out of airplanes.

My military entrance scores were good, so I was able to choose any Military Occupational Specialty that I wanted. I was looking for more than just a physical challenge, but my priority was a specialty that offered the maximum for college money. I found that mix in "13F": Fire Support Specialist, better known as a forward observer ("FO" for short) for the Field Artillery.[3]

I signed my contract on February 16, 2000, just two months after my eighteenth birthday, raising my hand to swear the oath of enlistment used for all branches of the Armed Forces:

> I [NAME], do solemnly swear (or affirm) that I will support and defend the Constitution of the United States against all enemies, foreign and domestic, that I will bear true faith and allegiance to the same; and that I will obey the orders of the President of the United States and the orders of the officers appointed over me, according to regulations and the Uniform Code of Military Justice. So help me God.

The primary allegiance of a soldier is not to a person—not to the president or a superior officer—but to the Constitution. Members of the military commit to defend the Constitution against all enemies, be they from outside or within the United States. Beyond this oath, Guardsmen also swear allegiance to their state and their governor.

A small minority of my fellow recruits chose to "solemnly affirm" rather than to swear. I, on the other hand, swore before God and implored his aid in my task of protecting and defending. I would be a

Christian soldier, whatever that meant.

The moment you sign your enlistment contract is when your military service obligation begins. Every Armed Service contract lasts no less than eight years. Even if you sign up for, say, three years of active duty, the enlistment contract still obligates you to five years of "Inactive Ready Reserve." At any time during that inactive period you can be recalled to service. This is a much-overlooked contractual obligation that catches a lot of new soldiers and their families off-guard.

Many recruits do not actually sign the contract and ship out to Boot Camp the same day. The period of time from signing to shipping is called the Delayed Entry Program, during which recruits do pre-training with the recruiting station command once per month on weekends. During that time they might earn advanced rank either for excelling in physical training (for the Army that included running, pushups and sit-ups) or for getting a friend to enlist alongside them.

In the weeks between my enlistment and shipping off to Basic Combat Training (also known as Boot Camp, or simply Basic), one of the candidates in that year's presidential election spoke candidly about his faith and how it paralleled his love for America and his military service. The rhetoric around faith and service were quickly overlapping in my life. My American and Christian identities, however indistinct they might have been before, blurred more and more into one. Boot Camp further entrenched the seeming singularity between church and state, giving me a new family, a new language, a new appearance—even a new name: Private.

Formation

✴

Undergoing the identity transformation of Basic with other young men was a test of endurance that the modern church could stand to learn from. In the earliest Christian communities, the process of becoming a Christian, called *catechesis*, took many years. It was physically traumatic (Christians were favored targets of state torture) and psychologically arduous. Catechumens were literally being indoctrinated.

Indoctrination has kind of a bad rap, but it shouldn't—at least within the context of church. Converts to Christianity are literally being taught to see the world through new eyes. The Latin words *doctrina*, for "teaching," and *doctor*, "teacher," describes the arduous process of catechesis. Discipling new converts should be serious business, and aiding others in entering and persevering in the journey Christ starts us upon can be a grueling process.

A catechumen had to completely relearn what it meant to be human. Instead of worshiping the state gods of ancient Rome, catechumens were taught that there was only one God. Baptism was associated with death in part because martyrdom was so prevalent among in the early church. Members of this "cult" were often sought out for capital punishment.

Like catechumens, new soldiers enter Basic and learn to see the world through new eyes—the eyes of a soldier, on the lookout for enemies of the Constitution both foreign and domestic. Whereas early Christian catechumens needed to be prepared for the possibility of their martyrdom—to be executed by the state—soldiers in Basic need to be prepared for the possibility of their death, or the death of others by their hand.

I had never thought very deeply about combat, at least not in any sense related to my faith. In my defense, nobody was talking about it at the time of my enlistment—nobody I knew of, at least. The United States had been at peace for nearly a decade; what reason did any of us have to think critically about what our faith had to say about killing for our country?

Basic would turn out to be a mere shadow of combat. Nothing in American culture adequately prepares a person for armed service: not movies, not books, not family heritage and certainly not Basic Training. Tim O'Brien, in his book *The Things They Carried*, said that you can tell a story about war is true "by its absolute and uncompromising allegiance to obscenity and evil."[4] There is nothing glamorous about combat. Nobody can really learn the reality of war except by living it; it's why we trust veterans more than journalists or screenwriters to tell us about it. The best that could have been done for me as a new enlistee—something recruiters notably don't do—would have been to provide a realistic portrayal of war, which as General Sherman famously said, is hell.

In order to withstand the sensory and moral onslaught of combat, military training entails desensitizing recruits. The product of this training is called "reflexive fire." Essentially, soldiers are trained to fire by reflex instead of by conscious thought. This is distinct from many law enforcement agencies, where trainees are taught to fire only if a target poses a credible threat. In military training, you repeatedly put down every target that pops up. The training process for new recruits is known in psychology as operant conditioning, which brings them as close to killing another person as possible without actually doing it. In order to achieve a particular goal (say, winning a war), the desired subject response (shooting enemies) requires overcoming normal behavior (in this case, human reluctance to killing) by reproducing stimuli in a way that distracts from whatever is preventing the desired behavior.[5]

The result of operant conditioning is that repetition can callous the individual to the moral challenge of war. It effectively hardens the hearts of service members and discourages moral clarity. This should trouble us, as reflexive fire is closely associated with post-combat depression and suicide. In the 2007 Emmy Award–winning documentary *Soldiers of Conscience*, West Point ethicist Lieutenant Colonel Pete Kilner insists that "in war, it's not that morality doesn't apply; in war, morality is *most* important."[6]

We usually associate the hard-hearted Pharaoh of Egypt in the book of Exodus with all kinds of evil—and maybe for good reason—but there also must be a reason that there are ten plagues and not just one. God gave Pharaoh ten chances to repent and let Moses' people go. But Pharaoh was stubborn, too invested in the status quo, to listen to God; his heart was numb to the plea of the Israelites.[7]

In Ezekiel 36:26, God promises to replace hearts of stone with hearts of flesh, but operant conditioning is akin to replacing our hearts of flesh with hearts of stone. And it's not only happening to soldiers. American media is replete with romantic depictions of battle, from *Band of Brothers* to *The Hurt Locker*. Marketing such profoundly personal experiences to a mass audience cheapens the pain of those who have actually experienced it. By subtly suggesting that combat is a place we can find honor, glory or revenge—or worse, entertainment—glamorous tales of warfare threaten to replace the hearts of flesh God has given us with hearts of stone (or maybe polished plastic). They embellish war, captivate our imaginations and condition us to disregard the incredible moral challenges that come with war.

I know that for me, by the time I found myself in that ambush in Najaf, my heart had done a great deal of hardening.

9/11 and 9/12

★

ON THE MORNING OF SEPTEMBER 11, 2001, I was in the dentist's chair at Ft. Bragg, North Carolina. I had just gotten back from the field after an airborne operation and a follow-on training exercise. I still had camo on my face while the dentist was pulling out a couple of teeth. When I got back to the barracks, I passed by the Fire Support office, where the forward observers gather between formations, and saw people fixated on a television screen with a picture of the World Trade Center in New York and a voiceover about a bombing. With the lidocaine and gas wearing off, I stumbled to my room, wondering why the news was running a story about an attack from all the way back in 1993.[8]

As guys in the hallway were yelling about going to war, I passed out in my bed. I didn't take much notice because by that point in my service, rumors of war were a recurring theme. During Basic Training the year prior, drill sergeants had rushed onto the drill pad screaming about the USS Cole bombing in Yemen. Fort Sill, where I was doing my initial training, had been locked down under the impression that war with Yemen was imminent. Nothing came of that—in retrospect, probably because the bombing occurred so close to a presidential election that would involve a change in administrations—so a year later I didn't expect anything to come of whatever the guys were yelling about.

A few hours later I woke up and went to pick up some pain meds for my gums. I made it out to my truck blissfully unaware of what was happening, but the radio must have been on, because in the truck I finally realized what was going on. I remember pounding my hand on the steering wheel, cursing loudly. I knew this time would not be just talk. There was no way this attack would go without a response. I was angry about the tragedy, but I also had a sense of trepidation at what I knew lay ahead. To be honest, I was also secretly excited about the prospect of testing my mettle on the battlefield. For me, like so many others in our country, the drums already beating thunderously for war drowned out the whisper of grief that we all needed so deeply to express.

I had been given time off after my dental appointment so that my gums could heal. So for three days, all I did was watch the news and listen to others in my unit make plans to get themselves to the front lines. We all wanted to go to war, everyone I talked to. Some were fueled by a desire for vengeance; others simply wanted to know what they were made of, to take the kid gloves off. My brigade (one of three in my division, the 82nd Airborne) would not have the opportunity to deploy to Afghanistan for at least a year, so I opted for reenlistment in order to pursue a program that would discharge me from my current contract while allowing me to retain all my benefits, at which point I would enter a contract with ROTC under full scholarship and return for a four-year stint as an officer. I was sure I could still deploy, but I would do so in a leadership position and with higher pay. It seemed like a win-win.

I reenlisted in August 2002 and made sure I got an assignment in Hawaii, where I had been accepted to Hawaii Pacific University. I was trying to make the most of the tuition assistance and free testing that active duty afforded, hoping to stay true to my implied promise to my parents that I would leverage my service to acquire a better education.

Home in California on transition leave, I called back to friends in my old unit. They didn't answer for a few days. I finally got an answer from another forward observer who had a penchant for embellishment. He said they were locked down, and that he wasn't supposed to be calling me. I didn't believe him at first, not until I heard another voice on the line yell at him gruffly to get off the phone.

My hardened heart sank. My old infantry unit ended up being part of the spearhead of troops that invaded Iraq in March 2003. I had left Ft. Bragg exactly ten days too early.

I thought I was missing out on something. I thought war was something to be pursued, something romantic and glamorous. I was wrong. God had other plans.

HAWAII

From the very beginning of my time in service, I had carefully cultivated my reputation. Physically and mentally, I excelled at the tasks I was given. In a social atmosphere that depends heavily on tangible accomplishments and visible markers of success, like tight haircuts and shiny boots, it was easy to do what was expected of me.

I came to Schofield Barracks on Oahu from one of the most prestigious units of the active Army—the All American Division, the 82nd Airborne. I was a paratrooper, which meant I wore my Airborne wings on my chest at all times. I was enrolled in Schofield's Air Assault School and came in first for the infamously grueling twelve-mile road march, beating an infantryman by nearly ten minutes. As an E-4 Specialist, I was already "double stacked," with two sets of wings upon my left breast; most "lifers" in the army don't achieve that feat until well into their careers.

I commanded respect from my peers, and not just because of what I wore on my chest. Just a few weeks before deployment, I was awarded an additional Army Achievement Medal by my artillery colonel, who, when I told him my time for completing the Air Assault road march, whispered in my ear, "That's a number you can be proud of, son."

Not long after arriving in Hawaii, my ROTC packet was put in, with enthusiastic support from the officers in my unit. The only snag was my shoplifting history; my record had been sealed after I attended a Scared Straight class, but it had come up in my background check during my delayed entry phase of recruitment. Would it prevent me from being accepted? I was advised not to worry about it, so I didn't. But I should have.

The packet came back disapproved, but the ROTC program director I was working with told me that a waiver would not be hard to acquire. I began putting together the required documents the same week my unit received their first deployment orders. I suddenly had a choice: deploy sooner rather than later, or get my education while I could.

The orders to war proved more compelling than the promise of an education.

Going to War

★

ON JANUARY 19, 2004, I WAS on the tarmac at Hickam Airfield looking outside at the plane that would fly us to Kuwait, our staging base for going into Iraq as the first replacements for the invasion force.

Logistical preparation is done well by the military, but very little moral prep work was done before we went off to war. You would have thought there would be some kind of framework given us through which we could understand what we were to do, but the "kill 'em all, let God sort 'em out" mentality had won the day. We knew about weapons of mass destruction, we knew about Saddam Hussein and the grave threat he represented, but nobody seemed to put much thought into how we would deal with the death we would encounter, our own or our enemy's.

I made it up as I went along. Staring down death didn't really seem too complicated. It essentially boiled down to the question of whether I was ready to die. The answer was no, but I might not have admitted it at the time. Somewhere in my mind, I decided that it would be easier if I died before I went to combat. In theory, I would be spared the emotional turmoil of thinking about my friends and family during my deployment, and a safe return home would be a kind of reward rather than a light at the end of a long, dark tunnel of fear and anxiety.

I committed preemptive suicide: I wrote a number of goodbye letters to loved ones, to be opened upon hearing of my death. It was torturous writing them, but I was convinced that it was the only way I could get through deployment in one moral piece; by knowing I would have the last word, I was stealing that opportunity from the "grim reaper" himself. In reality I was clothing myself in death.

This line of thinking was part of my baggage that bright January day in 2004. USO volunteers had given us all a small baggy filled with a miniature flag and a small note in Hawaiian that read, *Me Ke Aloha Pau Ole, A Hui Hou*—"With never-ending love, until we meet again." I thought it would make a great epitaph, as I was sure that I would see my friends and family again in heaven. The miniature flag was folded the same triangular way they do at military funerals, before they give it to the weeping next of kin. Before I got to Hickam, I had sent my box of death-letters to my dad, a next of kin, to distribute in the event of my demise. Death had disguised itself and walked aboard before I even boarded the plane; my actions included the emotions of a funeral, minus only the coffin.

ROLEPLAY FOR SURVIVAL

A crash course on infantry structure is in order:

- Four infantrymen are a *team.*
- Three teams (twelve men) are a *squad.*
- Three squads and leadership elements (forty-one men) are a *platoon.*
- Four platoons and leadership elements (about 190 men) are a *rifle company.*
- Three rifle companies and a headquarters element (about 860 men) are a *battalion.*
- A full *brigade* is made up of three infantry battalions and their attachments (including artillery, anti-aircraft, medical and other elements; about 3,100 personnel in all).[9]

The first several months of my battalion's deployment were un-eventful. We were assigned to a small airfield in a town called Tuz Kharmatu, south of Kirkuk, where our brigade was stationed. I spent a lot of my time in the early months of combat in our Tactical Opera-tions Center (TOC), assisting the fire support element in planning indirect assets and uploading all my CDs onto my computer. I was so bored I added about one hundred albums and all their information, down to each song's lyrics.

I know movies make you believe combat is all action and ad-venture, but that only describes maybe a tenth of the reality. In my experience, combat is essentially long stretches of unforgiving and almost painful boredom interrupted by brief and intense moments of sheer terror. But it's the terror that sells tickets and video games, so that's what makes it back to the home front.

That is not to make light of combat. I don't remember how many times the platoon medic and I beat the game in Call of Duty, but I do remember exactly how many times I fired my rifle using live rounds. I remember how many friends of mine acquired Purple Hearts. Those moments and memories are not easily lost. They are always items I recall in therapy sessions.

At one point in the middle of a lull in fighting in Samarrah in Oc-tober 2004, during Operation Baton Rouge, our platoon was required to have a session with a mental health specialist. No joke: in the midst of combat, we had a therapy session. We all sat in a room and talked about how we felt. In the middle of our surprisingly un-awkward session came an outburst from Sergeant Matthew Keli'i, a native Hawaiian so domineering that I always felt slightly on guard around him (even after we returned home and would go surfing to-gether). "I think we put on masks. We play a part we know is ex-pected of us . . . something we need to do in order to survive and get through it in one piece." Others nodded their head in agreement.

It was the first time I realized that I wasn't the only one that felt that way. We were all playing a kind of game, albeit a dangerous one. We had been planted in combat, and to make it to the other side—to home and to safety—we played our part.

In the documentary *The Ground Truth: After the Killing Ends,* a veteran of Iraq describes the situation of being put in combat: "You take a nineteen-year-old kid, give him a rifle and tell him, 'You want to go home to your girlfriend? Go destroy that city.'"[10] This is, of course, an oversimplification, but it viscerally describes the moral disarray of war. Just like negotiating the social space of high school, I was again engaged in a kind of roleplay, a coping mechanism in the absence of any reliable moral framework. We were all playing a part defined for us by society and circumstance.

In Philip Zimbardo's 1971 Stanford Prison Experiment (a study of roleplay under stress funded by the Office of Naval Research), students were given a prison scenario and assigned roles as either guard or prisoner. Those playing guards quickly became alarmingly brutal, and the prisoners surprisingly submissive, to the point of extreme duress. Zimbardo's *The Lucifer Effect* describes the experiment in more detail, a process by which "good people turn evil."[11] In another important (and equally controversial) study, Yale professor Stanley Milgram describes in his *Obedience to Authority: An Experimental View* a 1963 experiment in which participants followed the instructions of people in white lab coats, obediently inflicting what they thought was serious harm on another person.[12] Both experiments are critical to understanding how a person can come to do some of the things we expect of them in war.

We were all fulfilling roles that we had learned in movies and video games. It was like someone back home had the Xbox controller in their hands and we were just characters, responding dutifully to a gamer's keystrokes and flicks of the joystick. Until Sergeant Keli'i's comment, I wondered if I was the only one that felt like we put on our "war face" and played the part expected of us. Some of the guys would be markedly different in their rooms playing *Call of Duty* than they were when we "suited up" to go out on mission; outside the wire, there was a kind of detachment about them. Their regular character seemed to be deliberately put on hold while we went outside the wire;

game became reality and reality, a game. Dave Grossman, in his *On Killing*, claims that video games can act as a kind of operant conditioning.[13] When we found ourselves in battle, who was to say it wasn't basically a grandiose game of Cowboys and Indians?

After the ambush in Najaf, my role became reminiscent of Chris Taylor in the 1988 movie *Platoon*. I felt at risk of being "outed" as reluctant to return fire, even though there was no reason for me to think I would not have fired had I identified an "actionable target." In my mind I was doing exactly what was expected of me as a vigilant but discerning moral agent in war.

I was fighting the good fight the only way I knew how—with the wisdom of a serpent and the innocence of a dove. I was tempering my emotions by rational intuition, applying reason where there was nearly none. A Christian soldier, I thought, was slow to anger and had great understanding, since the quick-tempered exalts folly (Proverbs 14:29). I didn't have many exemplars of Christian combatants, but I did what I could to be a voice of compassion and discretion in my platoon.

At one point early in the fighting in Samarrah, an aged woman approached our platoon, holding her bandaged arm out to us. She was seeking medical assistance, since we were occupying the hospital and were not allowing anyone inside our perimeter. I remember taking her to the platoon medic and having to convince him to dress her wound, knowing we would easily get resupplied well before her local hospital would. I thought treating the woman was a no-brainer for medics—it's what they do—but "Doc" took some convincing. The medic was a good man; he just had to be stirred out of the collective moral superficiality we were all conditioned by. He eventually treated her and she went on about her way, and I left with a new appreciation for how inadvertently God can harden our hearts.

I went about my roleplay as Chris Taylor, knowing that on some level it was totally inaccurate and self-gratuitous, but having no other model upon which to base my self-restraint. Jesus, after all, never picked up an M-4.

Rescue Mission

★

LATE IN MY DEPLOYMENT, OUR company was tasked with supplementing another battalion southeast of Samarra. One night, my platoon was on a late night "rocketman patrol," during which we were supposed to be searching for opportunistic insurgents lobbing mortars toward our Forward Operating Base (FOB). We hadn't been hit for well over twenty-four hours, meaning any leads were dead cold. The point of patrolling was lost on all of us, including our platoon sergeant and lieutenant. Instead, we took turns manning the radio and watching for enemies (and friendlies who may not like us sleeping on the job).

Just after midnight, we got a distress call from another one of the units from our FOB. There had been a vehicular accident in a convoy headed back to base; a driver had rolled over an embankment above a reservoir.

Our Humvees roared to life and we booked it to the coordinates supplied by the medics. Our group of about twenty was the first to arrive on the scene, so we pulled into a perimeter with the vehicles from the original convoy. Half of the rolled vehicle, a Humvee that sat two in the cab up front and six in the open bed in back, was resting above the water inside a concrete enclosed reservoir. There were nine people in the back and three in the cab when the vehicle tumbled down about twenty feet to where it rested. Soldiers surrounded the wreckage, working to free the men in the cab.

The platoon leader, platoon sergeant, squad leaders, medic and I made our way down a mound that surrounded the site. As I carefully walked down the rock-strewn hill, past a medevac vehicle with its internal lights on, I saw a man inside being treated for a head wound. His entire face was covered in blood. Small droplets of bright red jumped from his lips and spattered the medic's face as he spoke. I remember it in slow motion, like in the movies. I'll never forget it.

As we continued down the short incline to the reservoir, we heard someone shriek, "I need swimmers to search the water!" At that, my pace quickened. I was one of the few men in my platoon who knew how to swim well; before we deployed, I had been encouraged to enroll in the selective Navy Diver course at Pearl Harbor. My unit knew I surfed regularly on the North Shore, a place where waves could get hairy. If there were anyone who could be trusted to search the water, it would be me.

The temperature was in the fifties on land, and I suspected the water was even colder. The concrete barrier was at least four feet above the surface of the water, so while I could get myself in the water, I would need to be hauled back up. I made sure there would be a constant presence that I could call on to grab me before I took off my boots and body armor, and I plunged in.

It was much colder than I expected. My breath escaped my lungs as I hit the water, and I gasped for relief and air as soon as I resur-faced. I tried to stay clear of what looked to be the rest of the dam and began to dip intermittently underwater, pointing my toes and hoping to hit the bottom of the reservoir—or a body. I was never so scared in my life—not of getting hurt or drowning but of having to retrieve a lifeless body from the frigid and foreboding waters. I prayed over and over to God that my search would be in vain.

Ancient communities once depicted hell not as fiery but frigid.

The devil, being far from God and the celestial bodies like the sun, was blue and cold. Dante describes one of the lowest levels of Satan's inferno as a frostscape, with whole bodies suspended in ice. Their heads alone remained above the surface for Virgil and his companion to stub and kick. I couldn't help but feel a bit like Dante, descending to a frigid hell in the fearful hope of finding friends to drag back to the surface.[14]

From the water, beneath the truck, I could see the person that most of the rescue effort was aimed toward. A sergeant had landed on the concrete wall of the reservoir before the vehicle did. His left leg was bent at an impossible angle, pinned by the weight of the Humvee. He had already been put on morphine and was muttering incoherently, whispering either sweet nothings or frantic pleas to his invisible wife. I couldn't bear to see his leg twisted well past its limits; the image of a layer of blood painting the concrete below him assaults my mind occasionally, and I cringe at every invasive thought.

The five minutes I spent in the water passed at a glacial pace. Eventually, the call was made that everyone was accounted for. I made my way toward the edge of the reservoir, but I couldn't lift my arms high enough for my friends to grab hold. It took a man on each of my arms to finally drag me out of the water.

Nobody had been lost. I was left blessedly empty-handed and with a supreme sense of accomplishment. I had done well; I had contributed to a successful rescue mission and faced a challenge few others in my platoon were able to. I was a good man, a selfless servant. I thought the worst was over, but I was wrong again.

Combat can be explained and retold by any number of fellow combatants—the blood and gore, the anxious anticipation of explosions and bullets, the overwhelming boredom between missions. All of it in some way is translatable by others in the martial fraternity. But none of the glamorous depictions and romantic sentimentality we put on war could prepare me for what came after the rescue of that cold November night.

Up until the rescue mission, I was more or less caught up in the generic feelings of patriotism that crystallized around the time I entered the military. I wasn't rampantly patriotic, but I also had no problem with conducting violence on behalf of freedom, democracy or America itself. I was a suspended pendulum, sitting comfortably on the patriotic side of the war and peace spectrum. Soon everything holding me in place, all the cultural and political assumptions I didn't even know I held, would fracture and break, sending me on a foreboding trajectory into unknown territory.

I Can't Save Everyone

★

BOTH THE VICTIMS AND perpetrators of combat lose people they love in war. The victims of war lose people close to them—people at home lose those they sent to combat, and those of us who see combat lose our fellow soldiers. But those who kill in combat also experience loss. Our loss is no less real than that of our victims. Many of us experience the very loss of ourselves.

After searching the reservoir I put my gear back on and began looking for other ways to help. I circled the vehicle, digging out the cab for a while, and occasionally helping the injured up the hill. I was in crisis mode, trying to fix things, everything. I hadn't even dried off; I was soaking wet in the midst of an Iraqi winter.

I kept passing someone I thought was a rescuer near the rear of the truck. I didn't take any notice until the umpteenth time I passed him, when I realized that his legs had never moved a single inch. I tapped his leg to get his attention. Nothing. I slipped my hand under his pant leg and felt for his skin. It was clammy, but I was sure I felt a pulse. I had found my next mission, the next thing I could save.

I hailed a medic, who shrugged. "He's too far gone. We need to focus on the men we can save."

My heart dropped, hard. In "the real world," that place we had left when we boarded the plane for Kuwait, medical personnel treat the most severe cases first. Priority goes to those who most need medical attention. Everyone else can wait. But in combat, triage is reversed; the direst cases with the least chance of survival are assisted only in dying painlessly. Medical supplies are rationed for those who are less injured and more likely to eventually return to the fight.

I have a stubborn spirit, and I wasn't about to give up on this fallen soldier. While gawkers piled up around us, I dug around the man's body using tools when they were available but continuing with my hands when they were not. The whole time I watched for his legs to twitch, to shift weight, anything to indicate he was stirring to life. I checked his pulse incessantly. Seconds turned to minutes, minutes turned to hours. Some joined me in my effort, but few stayed for long.

Sometime around 3 a.m., a convoy from FOB Warrior in Kirkuk arrived with a crane and a team of Special Forces medics. Only a few of the rescuers remained at the bottom of the pit. I watched from the bluff as they hooked the crane to the upturned Humvee, as the Humvee creaked and groaned loudly until it finally was lifted from the leg of the sergeant. He was now blithering much more loudly, paying no attention to the friend holding his hand as the wreckage scraped against his bare flesh, almost certainly causing more damage before the SF medics could go to work.

Nobody seemed to notice the other young man slipping toward the ultimate price, or my effort to prevent that from occurring. Nobody held his hand; nobody coaxed him to courage as he persevered through the ordeal. His body lifted slightly as the crane pulled up on the vehicle, and dropped softly when whatever he had been caught on was freed. It was not until that moment that one of the medics took notice and hovered over him to take his vitals. The medic's right thumb went up, a sign that the casualty was not yet a fatality. As he was taken away, I caught a glimpse of his face. It was ghastly grey, but there was a thumbs up! He had a pulse! I could cling to that at least.

My hope was dashed on the ride home. News came over the radio that the sergeant that was pinned would almost certainly face amputation and a ticket back to the real world. The young man I had tried to help had died on the way back to Kirkuk.

Back at the FOB, we had to spend the evenings in Blackout, which meant we could not use any lights in our military tents. Our platoon went to sleep in pitch black, but I couldn't find rest. My heart rate hadn't slowed since we got back. All I could think about was the dead black silence that surrounded that young man as he lay dying

The sun came up and we went to breakfast in the small mess tent. The cooks were showing *Pearl Harbor* on a television set in a corner by the chow line. We walked in right in the middle of the namesake scene, as Japanese bombers strafed the airfield along East Loch.

If I had had something in my stomach to throw up, I would have. I sat in a trance as everyone else around me ate. All I could think about is how human beings could watch fake gore, fake violence. I had seen death up close—right in my face. I had enjoyed this movie before I deployed, but now it was insulting and disgusting to me. All I knew was gone; all I thought I appreciated about war had eroded.

Over the next week, I continued to stare blankly into the pitch of night, unable to rest in peace in the crypt of our platoon tent. I wondered if the man could hear everyone around him. I wondered if he knew he was being ignored in favor of other, more viable casualties. Could he hear people clanging away at the vehicle, nowhere near where he was trapped? Could he hear my frantic clawing at the dirt around his legs? I hoped so. Maybe it would alleviate the survivor's guilt I was almost certain to encounter.

I questioned God. I doubted. Why did this young man die? Was he serving some greater purpose? He wasn't cut down heroically by enemy fire; he didn't throw himself on a grenade or sacrifice himself as a decoy to draw fire. He was sitting in the back of a Humvee packed with too many people when a fatigued and disoriented driver missed a turn. It all seemed so excruciatingly meaningless.

American culture taught me that death in combat was supposed to be honorable. It was supposed to tug our heartstrings and embolden us to fight on with the good and noble cause. Instead, my heart was clawed and dragged by nagging doubt and horrific memories. The worst was attending his memorial a day or two later. As we stood around the battle cross bearing his name, we heard the whistling of incoming rounds. They landed somewhere off target, nowhere near enough to cause us any real alarm. Nonetheless, every single person wandered off aimlessly without fully memorializing our fallen comrade. I kept looking over my shoulder as I followed the guys in my platoon off toward the horizon. I wondered if we were abandoning his memory as easily as we had his body to the dirt and the mud.

★ ★ ★

Somewhere in there, something struck me. Eleven months into my tour, I had seen a good number of bodies pile up. While I was on duty at a hospital in Samarrah, the morgue was filled past capacity. Bodies were left in black bags outside to swell and stink mercilessly in the desert heat. In fact, the number of bodies was greater than the amount of body bags the hospital had on hand. I was tasked with photographing them, in case their faces became disfigured in the desert heat, making identification difficult. I photographed countless dead and dying Arab faces. Not one tear tumbled down my face. They were not like me; their language, skin color and customs were all different.

What kept me from mourning the deaths of the Arab (and predominantly Muslim) people that I encountered? Was my heart that hardened? I thought I was a good man, fighting the good fight. I thought I was Chris Taylor in *Platoon,* always opposing the temptation to evil.[15] I wasn't torturing or humiliating prisoners like the trigger-happy sadists I heard about on the news. But when I looked at myself in the mirror I saw something different from before.[16] My experience revealed something I could not have simply learned on my own: I was a product of a systemically unjust and sinful world.

I had been formed by language and images and cultural markers that told me clearly who my enemy was. It only made it worse when I thought of how convinced I was that I hadn't been so formed. Conscience literally means "with knowledge." Knowledge is a one-way process; you can never unlearn the thing you come to know. Everything I thought I knew was coming under fire.

> Am I a good man?
> I thought I was . . .
> Everything is changed in this pale light
> That death has cast on all I've done.[17]

My experience at Samarrah was like finding a membership card to the Ku Klux Klan in my wallet—with my own signature on it. I could not believe that I could be so callous, so immune to the human cost of war.[18]

That week in November, my hardened heart broke in two. I saw just how deeply numb I was to the human suffering of the "other" that I saw every day in Iraq. I found that the thin red line between sinner and saint is not always so easy to discern, that the violence in the world is directly correlative to the violence in each of us.

One of my last memories in Iraq was in Mosul, during the first open democratic elections in that country. My platoon was assigned to a safe house overlooking a polling site in the old section of the city, where foot soldiers hadn't been yet. On election day, late in the afternoon, an insurgent threw a grenade toward our position. A young Iraqi soldier saved many of us from the brunt of the blast. The platoon opened fire, wounding the assailant considerably but failing to prevent his escape. I called in a medevac as our medic worked to stop the Iraqi soldier's bleeding, which was mostly superficial. Kneeling in the alley, I watched as blood spilled by our attacker mixed with the blood shed by our savior. Who was friend, and who was foe? They both bled red, like me.

That thin red line I had relied on to differentiate between sinner and saint pooled in the gutter at my feet. Is the line scrawled by a fine-tip marker, or painted with a rolling brush? A robust belief in original sin suggests we're all cast in a pale shade of red . . .

MOVEMENT TWO

"I think the human race needs to think more about killing, about conflict. Is that what we want in this twenty-first century?"

ROBERT S. MCNAMARA, SECRETARY OF DEFENSE
FOR PRESIDENTS KENNEDY AND JOHNSON

"This business of injecting poisonous drugs of hate into the veins of people normally humane, of sending men home from dark and bloodied battlefields physically handicapped and psychologically deranged cannot be reconciled with wisdom, justice and love."

DR. MARTIN LUTHER KING JR.

"Lord, I do not deserve to have you come under my roof. But just say the word and my servant will be healed."

ROMAN CENTURION OF GREAT FAITH (MATTHEW 8, FROM THE CATHOLIC MASS)

✯ ✯ ✯

The Good Fight of Faith?

★

ABRAHAM HESCHEL MARCHED with Martin Luther King Jr. to Selma, Alabama, and remarked that in so doing, he was "praying with his feet." When discussing the war in Vietnam, he was known to say that "in a representative democracy, some are guilty, but all are responsible."[1]

My conscience was constantly being tested, both under fire and under guard. It would take the wisdom of a serpent and the innocence of a dove to live a life that reflected the good in me that sin had tarnished. For over a year I had struggled with whether I was a good person. I wondered deeply and at times painfully over how I could go on living with the blood that stained my hands as an artilleryman in Iraq. God had done something that planted a seed of hope in my life, but I still wondered if I was a good man.

I didn't want to take too much or too little responsibility for my part in the war in Iraq. I did indeed participate in violence, but it was not quite my own violence. I was guilty, but *how*, and in what way? To whom could I actually be reconciled—to the entire nation of Iraq, to people I never saw upon whom my artillery fell from miles away?

I was a forward observer; I didn't always see the effects of the munitions I controlled. It was very likely I caused great harm, and even death, to people we encountered in 2004. But ultimately, I don't know. The first time I will find closure to that question that haunts me will be the Day of Judgment.

Was I a good man? I thought I was. In reading the Bible, I found that my story—our story—begins not with Genesis 4, the disobedience of Cain and the murder of Abel, but with the love and peace spoken into being by God in Genesis 1. We are created good; in fact we are called "very good" by God. How, then, does a good person fall to evil?

Foreshadowing
the Shadows

★

THE FIRST MEMORY I HAVE after watching the crack of thunder and puff of smoke was the platoon sergeant yelling in my ear to "Go! F***ing *go!*"

I was on a convoy from Kuwait to a small airfield in Tuz Kharmatu, not three days into combat, when the open-back Humvee in front of us took the brunt of an explosive blast less than one hundred meters away.

The gunner and passengers around him in the open cargo space of the Humvee had all slumped over. Maybe the driver too.

I crept forward; maybe I could force the Humvee out of the killzone if I nudged it from behind. It felt like forever before the passengers shook back to life out of shell shock from their first Improvised Explosive Device (IED) attack. In reality, it was just a few seconds.[2]

A little while after the attack, I found several large pieces of shrapnel lodged into the inch-thick plastic of a water can nestled just behind the driver's seat of my vehicle. The mirror on my side had a chunk missing. Based on the trajectory, several pieces must have missed me by mere centimeters. For some reason, I thought it was a good idea to send those shredded metal pieces home to my dad, mementos of his son's life nearly lost. I put them beside the miniature flag in the same tiny baggie I was given the day I boarded the plane for Kuwait. Families get caught up with war in ways nobody ever expects.

That night, I dreamt in color for the first time in my life.

I was on vacation with my three siblings. We were having a good time—lighthearted fun over drinks at a beautiful beach house somewhere. Things wound down and we made our ways to separate rooms in the house.

Lying in bed, I began to hear a ticking, like a clock. It was more than just sound; I could feel it all the way down in my flesh and bones. It was barely perceptible, but it picked up my heart and dragged it along to its increasing tempo. Like a fast train, faster, faster.

I grew frantic and rushed to the kitchen. At the last moment, I realized it was a time bomb. I made a mad dash for my little sister's room and reached the doorframe just as the explosion claimed her life.

I could feel all those pieces of shrapnel that could not reach me in life embed themselves in my skin. I could feel the acrid carbon powdering my face. I was paralyzed by shock, still gasping in paralyzing denial, when the ticking began again.

I put everything I had into rushing for my brother's room, words of warning just barely reaching my lips before his room exploded in a fiery blast like the one that had consumed my compatriots hours before, on the convoy. I was faster the next time, not waiting for the shock to overcome me before running straight for my older sister's room. But nothing could prevent the ticking, already at a breakneck pace, from reaching its consummation.

I woke in a sweat in the cool desert night. It would be three years before my nightmares would be diagnosed as a symptom of Post-

Traumatic Stress Disorder (PTSD).[3] During that time, I would also discover what it meant to be a Christian.

★ ★ ★

By the time I left Iraq, I thought I had had a pretty mild experience. Sure, there were the firefights and intense moments, but the majority of our time was spent watching bootlegged DVDs and playing *Tiger Woods Golf*. War might be hell, but it sure didn't feel that way all the time.

Early in our deployment, one of the guys in our battalion lost a valuable piece of equipment, so our mission changed from protecting a small airfield in a rural area south of Kirkuk to being a quick reaction force for the entire country. Starting in April, we lived out of duffle bags and spent nearly as many nights in our Humvees as we did on mattresses or in our sleeping bags. Because we moved around so much, we never got into any predictable patterns that the enemy could exploit to our disadvantage.

We were fortunate to have had only one fatality in our entire time in Iraq. Shortly before packing up to leave for Kuwait, my platoon got word that a soldier in our unit had died. Rumor had it he was playing Russian Roulette, a game in which you spin a revolver with a single bullet, put the gun to your head and pull the trigger. He had, apparently, gambled with his life and lost.

I suspected later that the rumor was a front to afford the guy some final respect. "Russian Roulette" was code for suicide; just playing it takes a certain level of suicidal intent. With less than a week before we were going to get home, he wanted to play games with his life.

It wasn't the only brush I would have with the dark and downward spiral of violence we had all begun. Of the three Non-Commissioned Officers (NCOs) that I served under in Iraq, one turned to crystal methamphetamine upon our return, and another—my own supervisor—attempted suicide several months later.

I wasn't immune to reckless behavior, which we are too often unwilling to ascribe to suicidal ideation. Some guys drive recklessly, others binge drink, a few get into narcotics. After my return from combat in 2005, I would go out to the North Shore, the epicenter of the surfing world, and surf in conditions I had no reason to believe I could handle. I can handle ten-foot faces at the most, but during those days I would take on waves about twice that size. I still remember the thousand-yard stare that would glaze over my eyes as I strapped on my bodyboard fins and velcroed up my leash. I wouldn't even be excited to be surfing; it was just a trope I was playing, another version of the enigmatic antihero marching off to near-certain death. It wasn't until years later, in counseling, that I was able (or willing) to call it what it was: I didn't particularly want to live. I didn't want to die, but I didn't feel alive. I was dead in the same way that I was before I deployed.

WAR IS HELL

I thought of my morbid pre-deployment letter-writing campaign as hedging my bets. Several of us got our affairs in order and told ourselves we were already dead. It seemed like the only way we could face combat with any semblance of sanity. The thinking went something like this: If I was dead before setting foot on the plane, then coming back home would be a bonus; if I was mortally wounded, the emotional cavern I would have to cross as I drew my final breaths might be shorter, more bearable.

My dad was a Vietnam veteran, so it seemed like something he could understand and bear. But it was a horrible and inconsiderate burden to put on him nonetheless. My symbolic death was as complete as it could be; tokens of my near-death, along with a folded American flag, had been sent to my next of kin. My living will had been written up and all my affairs were in order, just like the military trained me. I had figuratively killed myself and (literally) sent word back home; all I had to do was die *physically*.

Such morbid activity did not save me from the most horrible and haunting thoughts I would have in combat. Our platoon interpreter,

Qase, had seen *Bill and Ted's Bogus Journey*, the sequel to their more popular *Excellent Adventure*. The sequel has Bill and Ted visit hell, and the impression left on Qase was that the American notion of hell was to endure, into eternity, the most pain one could imagine. Since hell would apparently be different for each person, he asked me what hell was to me. So I described the hell that haunted me in combat.

"I'm sitting in the living room of my home, in California. The doorbell rings and I hear my mom come downstairs to answer. She takes no notice of me but goes to open the door, so I stand up to get a better view of her visitor. He wears an Army uniform and is accompanied by a chaplain. They have come to tell her of my death in combat."

"And how does she react?" he asks.

"Imagining her reaction *is* my hell."

"So, it happens again and again?"

"No, just once. That's all it takes."

★ ★ ★

Sometimes experiences melt into us so completely that they become instinct. We forget what it was like before a traumatic experience when it is so overwhelming in intensity or duration. We lose ourselves in the ocean of ambiguity that often surrounds events like a combat deployment.

Memories become reflexive when they guide our actions before we even have to think about them. If you witnessed a horrible car accident, maybe you become uncomfortable driving. If someone you know died in a plane crash, chances are you don't fly often. It was kind of like that for a lot of us coming home from war. On the bus from the airport to Schofield, I instinctively scooted away from the window as we passed a vehicle stopped on the side of the freeway. It was at that moment that I knew I had post-traumatic stress.

CURIOUS MORBIDITY

Learning to live with post-traumatic stress was easy at first; I ignored it almost completely. I had a lot to occupy my time, surfing the beautiful north shore of Oahu, flying with aviation buddies to other islands on a whim, hiking in the tropical rainforests surrounding Schofield.

My civilian friends in Hawaii knew I was in the military full time, but they connected with me through surfing, an activity that few of my Army friends shared with me. Surfing was my escape, a return to normalcy, I suppose, since I never saw myself making a career in the military. To my surfing friends, I was just "Logan," not "Sergeant Mehl-Laituri."[4] We would see each other all the time on the north shore at Pipeline, or on the south shore at Sandy Beach. Eventually we began to talk, and then we exchanged numbers. Before long, we were letting each other know where and when we were surfing and would grab a bite together after our session. Having these connections away from the military gave me some needed perspective. My civilian friends didn't really have any idea of what being in the military itself was like, and it drew me out of the mindset that I had built up over my years in service.

When I was getting ready to deploy, it was with my civilian friends that I spent my final moments. My last night in the real world was spent surfing well past dark, then eating a favorite Hawaiian dish for my last meal. I kept in touch with my friends while I was deployed, but I never burdened them with my most troubling experiences.

Shortly after I came home from Iraq, we were barbequing at a civilian friend's house in Kailua. We had a few drinks and were all feeling pretty relaxed. I guess that might be why one of them felt comfortable asking me if I had ever killed anybody.

· · ·

expression probably reflected that.
first time I had been asked. My mind lost its bearings, and my
The cursor in my mind was blinking on and off, on and off. It was the

· · ·

I loved my friends. I knew they didn't know any better. They didn't know how privileged that information is, how vulnerable and intimate it is, how deep our trust must be for me to even think about having that conversation. We had known each other for nearly two years if you count my time in Iraq, but it still wasn't enough.

People without combat experience can sometimes have a morbid sense of curiosity about killing. We watch our loved ones go into this black hole that none of us would want to face. The thought of it captures our imagination and our attention in a way that digs at us; we want to believe that war is like the movies, like the books and magazines.

Asking someone if they have killed is like asking them to detail their sexual encounters. Not only is it impolite; it hints at our shallow desires to be connected with something that has, in our modern Western culture, become sacralized. We want details, the pornography of images, but none of the pain and effort requisite of a healthy sexual relationship with an equal partner. We want anonymity; we want sterilized and emotionally safe dispatches from the front.

Perhaps I felt naked in front of the question, like my fig leaf had been ripped away. I felt like Cain, asked by God where his brother Abel was even though the Omniscient One knew quite well that Cain had killed his brother. What had I done to my brothers? From where was their blood crying out to God? Like Cain, I couldn't hide my guilt from the question.

Since then, I have been asked a number of times, and it hasn't gotten any easier. Often, I have learned, the question is being asked not out of curiosity but out of genuine concern. But still, casual conversation is rarely capable of drawing out such painful experiences in a healthy way. They must emerge without invocation, from a contrite heart, in trustworthy company. In the Roman Catholic tradition, this is known as confession and is elevated to a sacramental level; in more secular worldviews such interaction is often relegated to therapy. I am inclined to believe that a good friend might suffice, as I think a good, deep conversation in confidence with a trusted friend can be incredibly therapeutic, even sacramental.[5]

My friend, bless his heart, didn't know any better, and neither did I. I have either wisdom or foolishness to thank for holding my tongue. Maybe it was simply shame.

It wouldn't be the last time I would feel so exposed by having seen combat.

LOSING CONTROL

One of my best friends from high school planned his wedding to take place during my post-deployment leave in March. I was to be a groomsman. For his bachelor party, we had reservations at a hotel in Cancun, Mexico, and had made plans to go out to local bars that night and have fun as a group and say goodbye to his time as a bachelor.

As we were heading out to the bars, he started slapping me in jest. Trouble was, I wasn't really playing. When I struck him back, it was to return the favor, not to play in the game. But he was intoxicated, and he was the guest of honor, so he wanted to be humored.

I can't remember how it actually escalated, but he quickly became noticeably incensed, which in turn fed my own anger. What I do remember is having this sense of losing control, as if the person I knew myself to be was losing ground to something I wanted very much not to be. A kind of darkness was coming over me.[6] I began to lose sight of my friend; the whole world was slipping away from me. The neon signs around us seemed to dim, my peripheral vision narrowed, and our friends' voices became muffled and receded to the background.

Large crowds once gathered in the Coliseum in Rome to watch people get killed for sport. There is a story of an ancient martyr, Telemachus, interfering with the Roman gladiatorial games by running down the aisle screaming "In the name of God, stop!" The monk was the next to be thrown into the melee as a grisly spectacle. Telemachus may have been killed, but God vindicated him when Emperor Honorius, impressed by the monk's audacity, ended the games.[7] The monk's voice echoed somewhere deep in the pit of my stomach, before I lashed out at this person I cared for, before I totally lost control: "Logan; in the name of God, *stop!*"

I was naked once again; I had ripped my own proverbial clothes off. Maybe my friends hadn't noticed, but all that baggage I was stowing away had been exposed by my near failure to keep my composure. I knew immediately that I could no longer participate in the evening's festivities.

It took a lot of energy to keep myself from giving in to my anger, to refuse myself the satisfaction of revenge on my friend. The other groomsmen tried to convince me to hang out and have fun, but I was too far gone. It took two hours of pacing angrily on the beach by our hotel before I calmed down. When they returned hours later, they insisted that I had made a mistake by not just "letting it all go." The mistake would have been precisely that, though: to "let it all go" would have added physical scars to the spiritual ones I already carried.

The Seeds
of Discipleship

☆

I DON'T TRUST MY OWN opinions about myself. Even Sigmund Freud, the father of psychoanalysis, suggested that you cannot analyze yourself. You really can't know yourself without others telling you who you are. You can't grasp exactly how much of a saint or a sinner you are without the insight of honest friends. In intimate relationships, I think you can learn even more; the increased vulnerability lends itself to greater honesty.

While in Honolulu after Iraq I went to a house party at a friend's place. I met a wonderful woman there, Thena Jenkins, who would be my first committed relationship, one in which I learned who I could be.

Thena's name came from the Greek *parthenia*, for maidenly. She was a military "brat"; she had lived in places around the world as her dad was assigned to one of the seven-hundred-plus U.S. military bases around the world. The Jenkins family had retired to Hawaii a few years prior, and Thena was enrolled at the University of Hawaii, where her brother, Nathan, was also a campus minister. She was studying marine biology, and her hair was already bleached from many days in the salt and sun, freckles marking her fair skin. She would talk endlessly about oceanographic stuff, but all I had ears for was the science behind waves and ocean currents. At the party, she and I must have been the only two not drinking alcohol—she because of her evangelical upbringing, I because I would have to drive an hour back home to the North Shore.

Eventually, Thena invited me to her family's house for dinner and their weekly Bible study. I had come to expect that Bible studies be based on selected texts of Scripture, so I initially brought a study Bible with me. I learned quickly that her father, Theodore (who insisted I call him Ted), had a penchant for putting things bluntly, something he certainly learned as a First Sergeant, the highest-ranking person in a company-sized Army unit. As we sat to eat, he told me that he did not care for military personnel.

"Excuse me?" I coughed, nearly ejecting some Korean chicken from my mouth.

"Yeah, I've seen it all. You Joes are trouble," he returned casually.[8] My chopsticks paused mid-carry while my eyes darted left to right, wondering if I was the only one who heard the comment. This was not the kind of conversation that is carried out between parents and the guy their daughter is dating, was it? Was this some kind of trap? I had absolutely no social bearing. So I said nothing. I kept pulling food from plate to mouth in as fluid a motion as I could with my poorly developed chopstick skills.

It was not an uncommon sentiment on Oahu, where military personnel often have a (not always undeserved) reputation for recklessness and debauchery. It made me wonder if he held the same opinion while he was overseeing the lives of the two hundred or so personnel in whatever unit he had retired from. The Jenkinses were all pretty enthusiastic in their faith, and it made me wonder if there was a conversion experience post-service that included some kind of disaffection from the military.

Ted continued as I chewed awkwardly.

"But, you know, I think God wants me to learn a lesson. Thena has never dated a soldier, so this will be a lesson in humility for me."

He felt that God was teaching him something in having his daughter date a soldier. What was I supposed to do with that? You don't follow up "I don't like you" with "But God is in this," do you?

I looked at him blankly, waiting for the ball to drop, for him to crack a smile and let out a hearty laugh, keying me into whatever inside joke he was establishing for us to laugh about later. He never did. He was totally serious. I glanced at Thena, who smirked innocently with an expression that suggested, "I could have warned you, but . . ."

I would continue to eat regularly with the Jenkins family. The theological extent of the weekly "Bible studies" was for everyone present to reflect on the same question: "What is God doing in your life?" I hadn't had a Bible study like that before. In youth group culture, I had been inundated with self-gratifying trivialities and irrelevancies, like how many marshmallows I could stuff in my mouth. The closest we got to theologically relevant discussions were one-way conversations during which we listened but were not trained to question. Sure, we had questions, but they were about the text, the circumstance of the Gospel stories. We were not trained to wrestle with God like Jacob did; we were not encouraged to ask deep questions of God like Abraham often did. Bible study had meant sitting around talking about a certain text, chosen the week prior, rarely moving much deeper than the text itself. With the Jenkinses, by contrast, I was forced to think of God in active terms. They made me consider not merely that God acts each and every day, but that our lives are contingent on the life of God. Considering the question every week forced me to see my life in light of God, instead of vice versa.

I cannot overstate how transformative the question was for my faith. By exploring what God was doing in my life—how it was my life that was entered, and not vice versa—I learned how to explore my relationship with God in a way that was not reductive or superficial. Before, I simply assumed God would make himself known.

Now I was forced to look for God. If I was simply waiting on God, it was not my fault when I felt nothing. But by seeing God as active and engaged, the tables were turned; if I didn't find God, maybe I was looking in the wrong places.

FOLLOWING JESUS WITH MY HEART *AND* MY HEAD

My occupation in the Army demanded I use my head. I worked a lot with geometry, practiced timing and built up attention to detail. Because we controlled indirect assets, we had to have honed spatial skills; if we plotted the map poorly or timed bombardments incorrectly, it could cost my unit their lives. It was challenging, but I excelled *because* I felt challenged.

My experience of the church up to that point, by contrast, hadn't been challenging; it had been accommodating. It hadn't offered anything constructive to say about the direction my life took; my impression was that if I wasn't violating rules (by using drugs or having premarital sex, to name a few), church wasn't interested in me. Trying to shape a life based merely on what not to do is a frustrating and confusing endeavor.

Having a model of a more deliberate discipleship, of shaping one's life more tangibly around the Gospels, enabled me to think about Jesus in more concrete terms and opened up the world of the Bible to me. God became more present to me because I was able to think critically and question my less developed beliefs. Of course, I was not drawing God closer myself, but rather I was being *drawn to* God.

I still wrestled viscerally with my combat deployment. Sometimes at night I would wake with a start in a sweat. On the good nights, I would be left wondering what it was that had startled me so. Other nights, I knew all too well the gory details—the sights, colors, smells and emotions that convincingly wrenched me back to the battlefield. The question revisited me often: Was I a good man? I thought I was . . .

★ ★ ★

I had begun regularly attending a nondenominational church in Haleiwa, where I lived off base, on the north shore of Oahu. First Christian Church of Oahu gathered Sunday mornings in the local community center, an old gym with big slat windows and double doors that were left open during the service to allow the tropical breeze to lift our spirits and fill our nostrils with scents you can only find this side of heaven. It was in worship times before the sermon that I began to feel a connection with God I hadn't felt since high school. There in the back of the room, I would sway and sing, close my eyes and let myself inhabit the moment. I remember quite clearly weeping in some indescribable sense of relief.

I would spend all week on base, dealing with everything the military throws at you. I had been transferred to another unit because ours was being transformed to a medium mechanized unit, a Stryker Brigade. To remain with the unit meant you had to reenlist, which I had no intention to do. Only ten months were left on my military contract, and I had tunnel vision for getting started with college. Instead, a number of us were sent to the other infantry brigade, which would retain the "Light" designator, which basically meant dismounted, instead of armored, infantry.[9]

In the midst of that move, I also had put in to drop ninety days off my termination date. The day my discharge from active duty was scheduled to occur[10] would conflict with me starting school at Hawaii Pacific University in time for their fall semester, so I had requested a school drop before I left the unit I deployed with. In the midst of this unit move within the Army, I already seemed to have one foot out the door.

Pride and
the Wrong Side

✭

THAT FALL AND WINTER WERE characterized by reading, learning
and internal conflict about my faith and service. I had enrolled in a
New Testament history class at Wayland Baptist University satellite
campus in Honolulu. For the first time, I was taught how to dissect
and explore the Gospels, to have a peek inside and get a feel for what
they were saying. Our textbook was the NIV Study Bible, and it was
the only book that was assigned. I hadn't read the Bible seriously
since I was in grade school, because it was forbidden in homeroom
reading period. I was a stubborn kid sometimes. But this time I wasn't
reading to tick anyone off.

During one class we discussed the Passion of Christ. On overhead
slides the professor displayed an article that illustrated a historical
perspective: the common practice of flogging in Rome and its effect
on muscles of the back, why Jesus bled blood and water in the cross,
how victims of crucifixion suffocated, and why Roman practice was
intended to torture its victims and intimidate onlookers. The Bible
became more than just a book to me in those classes. I remember

sitting on my tailgate talking to other students long after class wrapped up. Tuition was covered by the military; I was literally getting paid to learn about Jesus.

In very short order, though, things started to get really messy. I began realizing that the men that arrested and flogged Jesus were soldiers. The men that nailed his hands to the cross were centurions doing their duty. I felt like a bad guy all over again, being escorted to the back seat of a squad car as the Holy Spirit slapped some heavy conviction on my heart . . .

I had watched friends taunt and assault detainees for no reason, just like the soldiers that mocked Jesus and crowned him with thorns. During Operation Baton Rouge, in October 2004, I had watched as another soldier punched a handcuffed Iraqi police officer in the stomach just because he could. I watched frozen and spellbound, betraying my comrade (and his victim) by my silence. While in Iraq, I hadn't just sat in a guard tower; I was on patrol, calling for fire, planning missions, barreling recklessly through villages in the driver seat of a Humvee.

How could I claim Christ? I was the person *to whom* Christians were supposed to turn the other cheek, *with whom* they were supposed to walk a second mile, heavy laden with *my military gear*. I could not escape the feeling that I was on the wrong side of Christian history.

Soldiering in the New Testament is a difficult subject to interpret. Great power carries with it great temptation; the power to kill is easily, though not always, abused. It was well within soldiers' authority in the first century, for example, to ask a civilian to carry combat gear (Matthew 5:41), but gambling for a condemned man's clothes and striking him in the face were not (Matthew 27:27-31; Mark 15:16-20; Luke 23:36). Crowning a man with thorns and dressing him up as a head of state (Luke 23:11) piled insult upon injury, and we are rightly incensed by the obscenity. But temptation is there, and the hell of war easily disguises occasional acts of mockery and torment. In Iraq, it was horrifically common to desecrate bodies, dead or alive.

But if there is tragedy in combat, there is also beauty; profanity exists in the shadow of the sacred.[11] Jesus himself praises a commander for his faith (Matthew 8; Luke 7); to this day the centurion is quoted at every Catholic Mass, moments before the priest consumes the Holy Eucharist: "Lord, I am not worthy that you should enter under my roof, but only say the word and my soul shall be healed." It is a soldier who observes Jesus hanging on the cross, bleeding and apparently beaten, who becomes the first to confess, "Surely [Jesus is] the son of God" (Matthew 27:54; Mark 15:39; cf. Luke 23:47). It is well known that the soldiers in Luke 3:14 have done nothing to warrant a condemnation from John the Baptizer, and we know that Cornelius, in Acts 10:2, was "devout and God-fearing . . . and prayed to God regularly," practicing charity with his family. Felix, "who was well acquainted with the Way" of Jesus, made sure his men gave Paul some freedom so the apostle's needs could be taken care of (Acts 24:22-23). Centurions valiantly protect Paul in Acts 21:32 and stay with him until his death in Acts 28. The martial fraternity, as it were, is not entirely bad.

It was soldiers performing their martial duties, however, who aided in arresting Jesus at Gethsemane (John 18:12). Religious leaders would not have had anything to do with the crucifixion itself, which fell within the state's ordained authority for punishing insurgents and insurrectionists (the claim leveled against Jesus). In fact, John unequivocally states that "*the soldiers* crucified Jesus" (John 19:23, emphasis mine). A soldier would not have been court-martialed for nailing Jesus' hands to the wood of the cross at Golgotha any more than a prison guard would be for administering a lethal injection at San Quentin. Most, if not all, however, are forever altered by the performance of those duties, no matter their legality or justifiability. The door through which you go in taking a life doesn't remain open behind you; the threshold cannot be uncrossed. It alters your very consciousness; the truths you learn about yourself can never be unlearned.

I thought PTSD was hard to deal with, and it most certainly was, but it paled in comparison to the harrowing of my conscience, to the great guilt I was feeling for being a "Christian soldier." I felt so stupid for not seeing it earlier.

We were reading the Gospel of Luke in class. I was fascinated by a parable in Luke 18, where a Pharisee and a tax collector are simultaneously praying—the tax collector for mercy, the Pharisee in praise of himself. I was learning, the hard way, how much I resembled the Pharisee. I was thrown into moral and theological disarray as my entire framework for understanding God began to melt away.

I had been in the Army nearly five years by that point. I had taken more than my fair share of silver coins from the establishment. I learned, more and more each day, that

> I'm just another Judas, kiss your face
> While I drive the nail through your hand . . .
> My sin yelled "Crucify!" louder than the mob that day.[12]

"Woe to you hypocrites," we say, echoing Jesus, as though we don't know what it's like to be deceived by our own good intentions. For all the talk about being a sinner that I heard as a youth, nothing had prepared me for the reality that Iraq confronted me with. Musician Derek Webb has pointed out that "until you are a real sinner with a real savior, you will be a hypothetical and theoretical sinner [with a] hypothetical and theoretical savior."[13]

Iron Sharpening Iron

★

GOD WASN'T DONE WITH ME though. I was attending church regularly and taking my faith seriously. I was opening myself to the movement of the Spirit, even if, in that time in my life, the Spirit had nothing nice to say to me. I was committed to living more fully into the life of Christ, to not merely *confirming* him but *conforming* my life to his.

The biggest log in my eye at that point was my professional expectation to "kill 'em all, let God sort 'em out." When Jesus told his followers to love their enemies, I realized, he certainly did not intend for that love to be expressed at the business end of an artillery shell.

My New Testament classes conflicted with the Jenkins Bible study dinners, so I began going to another gathering Thena had suggested. The Bible study groups put on by the Salvation Army in Honolulu were more reminiscent of the ones I had been to in my youth, but I went into them with much more enthusiasm, given my newfound interest. It was in these settings that my faith really started to take off.

A man named James Yamada Jr. led a weekly get-together of mostly down-and-out locals who came for free food and meaningful fellowship. Yamada preferred to be called Junior or Uncle Jimmy. He was nearly twice my age, so I opted for the latter. Like a number of locals on Oahu, Uncle Jimmy spoke in Hawaiian Pidgen and always had a big smile on his face. His hands were weathered but gentle. He was the son of an electrician who had found Jesus relatively late in life, and he used the same hands for guiding thick electric cables and to pat friends on the back and hug neighbors in need. Jimmy managed a company that had contracts with major construction projects across the state, so he was always offering material as well as spiritual support. He had more money than he let on, but he was always reminding people that it wasn't his, but God's. If a friend was in need, it was God providing, not his wallet. It was so different from the vain and conspicuous affluence I was accustomed to from my youth.

I gravitated to Uncle Jimmy. He was very vocal in his faith, and he never took off the righteousness in which he was clothed. He was becoming a kind of spiritual mentor to me, guiding me along the road of discipleship.

My brother Evan had attended the same youth group I did when he was in high school before going on to study philosophy at a nearby college, and he had told me at some point that he was a Christian. After my deployment he had come to Oahu to live with me. But he and I had grown a little distant; he was having trouble finding a steady job, and the emotional toll was clear to both of us. I went to Jimmy about how to bridge that divide. He told me to pray.

One evening, I figured our common faith might be a welcome relief from an argument Evan and I were having. "Before we part ways," I asked, "can I pray for us?"

He paused, looking at his nails. "No," he said abruptly, without eye contact.

I wasn't sure how to respond to him. I'd never been told I was not welcome to pray with another Christian.

"What?" I blurted out, flabbergasted.

Another pause.

"You only let God into the conversation when it's convenient to you. I think it's disingenuous."

With that, he retreated to his room. I sat in ponderous silence for many moments before realizing that he was absolutely right. I was praying for things that benefitted me, for God to give me things that satisfied my own desires or expectations. How meaningful can prayer be if we're only ever asking for parking spots or to pacify debates? I was selectively depending on God; I was not giving my entire life to him.

I discovered slowly that I needed to either reimagine my professional trajectory—blowing stuff up as a forward observer for the artillery—or stop calling myself a Christian. I knew now, after my brother's challenge, that Jesus meant nothing if he wasn't everything. Being a Christian soldier meant I was to ultimately obey God, rather than the officers appointed above me.

I poured my energy into trying to learn about what the church has taught about war and peace. I began asking every Christian I knew about the challenge of evil and the individual Christian's obligation to the state. Of course, my questions were not as decisive as that. I usually would ask simply if I, as a Christian, could serve in the military and be expected to kill enemies I was commanded to love. Would being a Christian preempt me from martial service, or was there a way to serve both the cross and the sword?

★ ★ ★

Not long after coming home from Iraq, I was promoted to sergeant, a non-commissioned officer (NCO) rank. One of the central parts of being an NCO is to develop new privates into leaders, to eventually become NCOs themselves. My first such assignment, Private Anthony Gallo, had just come from basic training and was an eager learner. He was so excitable that he always insisted on calling me "Sergeant Mehl-Laituri" instead of just "Sergeant," or the even more common "Sar'nt". He was even more excited about being a forward observer and absorbed information like a sponge.

Anthony hailed from New York City, and he was a devout Catholic. In fact, he told me he had considered the priesthood before finally enlisting in the Army. Tall and well-built, he was a typical Italian. His hair, particularly his eyebrows, made me wonder if he used hair dye, which was weird because he couldn't have been older than twenty.

Exceptional performance in Basic had earned Anthony a promotion to E-2. I looked forward to mentoring this new squared-away young soldier in the same ways I had been brought up: to value loyalty, respect and compassion. Little did I know that Anthony would have some things to teach me as well.

Perhaps tragically for Anthony, he arrived in the midst of my spiritual tumult. I think I did a decent job keeping the thick of it from interfering with my duties, but I am also a fairly trusting person, and my thoughts often pour out of me verbally. More than once I mentioned to him the things I was thinking through. Thankfully, talking with Anthony never descended into heated debate; we had enough respect for one another that we wouldn't stereotype each other in order to make a point.

Eventually, our conversations turned to theological justifications for violence in the face of evils like the attacks of September 11, 2001, and those that Iraq dictator Saddam Hussein had perpetrated against his people. Anthony was very familiar with Catholic teaching and directed me a number of times to the Catechism of the Catholic Church. He was no pacifist but believed strongly in the tragic necessity of violence, which was good because he probably could have put a hurt on me in "combatives" training we did with the infantry. If he had had doubts about violence, he would not have enlisted several months earlier.

What Is It All About?

★

OF COURSE, I WENT TO UNCLE Jimmy with questions as well. I knew I could ask him anything. During one particularly trying time with a friend, I went to Jimmy and asked what he thought would be wise. His response, one which was repeated to me innumerable times in the course of our relationship, was summed up in three simple words: "It's about love!"

At first, that reply was frustrating. It forced me to consider what the most loving response was to whatever situation I faced. Sometimes it required a level of patience and compassion I wasn't sure I possessed.

Love forces us to slow down and sympathize. To love is not always the most expedient action—it might not even be the most rational—but Christians are not called to efficiency or rationality. Jesus calls the church to love; it is the very thing by which the world will know us (John 13:35).

I would sometimes be left annoyed by his repetitiveness, but Jimmy was right every time; it is about love. So when I approached him to ask about military service, I knew he would remind me of the centrality of love and maybe help me think through the most loving response to the urgent situation in which I found myself: my new unit had received orders to Iraq, meaning I was facing a second deployment.

I met with Jimmy in his office in downtown Honolulu on a day I had off from work. He listened for a long time as I articulated what I had learned in the New Testament class and the conversations I was having with Anthony. When I felt like I had said everything related to my struggle that far, I let out a sigh and stopped.

Jimmy rocked in his chair a few times, considering it all. His hesitation was not characteristic of our other conversations. All of his encouraging words to date about the centrality of love had reinforced my awe and fear of God; they were like scaffolding surrounding my heart as it went through renovations. But now his words were like a worker's sledgehammer, taking out an entire section of scaffold. The United States military, he speculated, was "probably God's hand of judgment in the Middle East."

I tried my best not to show surprise, but I felt my stomach sink. I waited for him to explain how he squared his injunction to love with my being an instrument of God's wrath, but it never came. He reasoned that the Ten Commandments forbade "murder," not "killing," that the two were theologically distinct.

Jimmy's theology, in at least the way he expressed it to me, is what many theologians call "holy war." Holy war theology claims that God himself commands violence in order to overcome evil. Christians are to fight fire with holy fire, force with righteous force. It would not be the last time I would be encouraged to think about whether God did or does command violence as part of the divine plan, and nearly every time it relied on accounts from the Old Testament, almost never from the Gospels or Epistles.

I tried my best to consider if what I did in Iraq had any divine purpose. It has been said that war is an attempt at ordering chaos, just as God did cosmically at creation. But it has also been said— more accurately, in my opinion—that war is hell. It certainly felt that way to me, so I couldn't bring myself to agree with Jimmy that God would bless war as readily as we expect him to.

Learning a
New Bad Word

★

DURING MY CONVERSATIONS with various acquaintances, I came across the term "conscientious objector" (CO). I had heard it maybe half a dozen times in my life prior to 2005, and they were always derogatory references. Particularly with my military experience and conditioning, I was averse to conscientious objection. I associated objectors with draft dodgers. But the term kept making its way into my conversations nevertheless.

One day, another forward observer I knew, who had deployed in a different infantry battalion on the same 2004 combat tour, told me he was applying to be a CO. Perhaps only because I had softened to the term in the course of my conversations about war and peace, I entertained him as he went on about the process for application.

The procedure for applying to be a conscientious objector is outlined by a regulation unique to each branch of the Armed Forces (all drawing from the authority of Department of Defense Directive 1300.6). The various regulations are constantly being revised and updated with mostly minor changes.[14] I had some experience with regulations during time in the Battalion TOC in Iraq, so I knew some of the language and how to negotiate the legalese. I downloaded a copy of the CO regulation and read it one night at a coffee shop in Mililani, far enough away from base to not be noticed by others in my unit. I knew my interest would not be taken to very keenly.

The application seemed fair enough. The service member, by articulating their sincere objection to war in any form, could get an honorable discharge if they continued to serve uprightly during the process. It was like the person and the Army mutually agreed to terminate the enlistment contract.

What was I to do? With my time on active duty and the esteem I held for other service members, I did not feel satisfied considering discharge. The military is like any other institution; it is less about the institution than it is about the individuals who make it up. All I knew of the military was the people I encountered, and a large number of them I deeply admired. Moreover, I found very little satisfaction in the two ideological extremes—strict obedience or absolute objection—currently available to me. Without any substantive theological training, I didn't know how to respond in faith to the call to love my enemies, even those that my country expected me to be prepared to kill. Jesus seemed to be beckoning me to an allegiance greater than those I had known before; sharper than the crispest salute and closer to my heart than any hand during the national anthem.

Epiphany

⭐

By April, preparations for my unit's deployment were well underway. We were scheduled to train for a month in Ft. Irwin, California, at the National Training Center. We boarded buses at Schofield, bound for the airfield at Hickam, where we would get on planes to fly to California. Anthony sat behind me a few rows and across the aisle, back erect, eyes alert, sticking out from the rest of us like a German Shepherd in a pack of tired, droopy hound dogs.

Several of us had gotten up early to prep our bags and, ready to catch up on lost sleep, had our heads propped against the seat in front of us. In my ears rested earphones connected to my MP3 player; music had long been a means of contemplation for me, and the brief moment of serenity allowed my mind to drift to my theological conundrum.

Despite my exhaustion, I feverishly considered what God would have me do. Ask to get out as a conscientious objector, opting for discharge and severing the ties I shared with the brave men with whom I served? Or deploy as planned, onward, as a Christian soldier to war?

My thoughts raced and question piled high upon question, concern upon concern. My mind wandered precariously toward confusion and exasperation. The tempo of the music picked up on pace with my thoughts, quicker and quicker . . .

Then something happened. With my mind racing around in circles, continuously questioning and querying, it seemed as though an unseen force redirected its frantic energy—like my mind got caught in a boomerang in mid thought, slowing at first, before finding its path. My inner voice, my pondering inner monologue, ceased. In an instant, I saw myself in the third person. I was in the Middle East, in a war-torn world I was all too familiar with. I had walked this land, weapon in hand and at the ready, two clicks from "safety" to "burst." In an infantry platoon, you do not leave your weapon. Under any circumstances. It is an instinct hammered into you by sheer force of will; your weapon is your life. A rifle is like a belly button—so much a part of you that you might not think of it constantly, but you would know if it was missing. To be without it would leave you feeling as exposed as if you had walked off without your right hand.

But there was no weapon in this vision of mine.

Had I not already been to combat, the significance of this vision would have escaped me. But I had been to combat, and at one point I had left my M-4 in my room while I went to take a shower when, two steps outside the building, I was dumbstruck by shock: how did I get that far before remembering my rifle?

The vision must not have lasted even a split second, but it could have been an eternity. I had a sudden, crystal-clear sense of confidence:

The battle fought
The war is won
The devil done
God's kingdom come
Jesus has won
Jesus has won
God's kingdom come[15]

I sat up immediately in the bus, hands searching frantically for a pen and paper. My job always required pens, which I had in spades, but paper was hard to come by at that moment. I stumbled upon three receipts in my wallet, and I began jotting down the thoughts darting through my head.

I knew from reading the Army regulations regarding conscientious objection that this was my "crystallization of conscience," the moment at which one is no longer able to support "war in any form." Our consciences likely never stop maturing, of course, but military regulations require applicants to describe a moment of crystallization of conscience as a demonstration of their sincerity. So I recorded the date and time precisely: 9:40 a.m., April 20, 2006.

In my reading of the Army regulation, I found what I figured must have been an administrative oddity. According to the regulations, there were actually two ways of being recognized as a conscientious objector. The most prominent form of objection was to seek discharge, known in the military as "1-O status." But there was a second, less common status identified as "1-A-O," which was to continue military service as a noncombatant conscientious objector.

I had not given 1-A-O much thought primarily because I figured it was a typo; in Boot Camp it was made abundantly clear that, basically, there are no noncombatants, that "every man is an infantryman first."[16] Although our mission in Iraq was by then, at least ostensibly, to "win hearts and minds," we seemed to have forgotten that the art of persuasion looks nothing like the art of war. Noncombatant CO status notwithstanding, there is no legal (or, in the case of military, regulatory) protection for someone who wishes to serve bravely but nonviolently on the field of battle.

I looked back at Anthony, who had seen me perk up. I handed him the slips of paper I had scrawled my thoughts on. He reached in his pocket and pulled out another receipt in response, affirming that I had "discerned [my] own special spiritual vocation from God by extensive prayer and meditation."

Anthony provided the context for what I was experiencing. Ministers often speak of their calling, the moment or series of moments during which they heard God call them to their own unique field of ministry, their vocation. My brief flash of clarity was like that— God's way of giving me a compass and pointing me in the direction I was to go.

My commission from God was clearer to me than anything had ever been before in my entire life. I would seek 1-A-O status; I'd pursue any and all means to return to Iraq without a weapon. I was just naive enough to think it could work.

MOVEMENT THREE

"The future of modern society depends much more on the quiet heroism of the very few who are inspired by God. These few will greatly enjoy the divine inspiration and will be prepared to stand for the dignity of Man and true freedom and to keep the Law of God, even if it means martyrdom or death."
DIETRICH BONHOEFFER, LUTHERAN PASTOR MARTYRED
IN NAZI GERMANY

"War will exist until that distant day when the conscientious objector enjoys the same reputation and prestige that the warrior does today."
JOHN FITZGERALD KENNEDY, CATHOLIC WWII NAVY VETERAN,
ASSASSINATED PRESIDENT OF THE UNITED STATES

"Father, forgive them, for they know not what they do."
JESUS, DURING HIS EXECUTION (LUKE 23 ESV)

✯ ✯ ✯

Conscientious Objection, or Something Else?

★

ARRIVING AT FT. IRWIN, California, I had to consider how to reconcile my newly crystallized conscience with a month of combat training. Because I had well over five years in the military at that point, I knew I would be learning little new. Furthermore, I would not actually be harming or killing anyone, and possibly not even simulating such an event. At that point in the Iraq War, training had begun to focus on the mission of "winning hearts and minds." Deliberate, intense combat scenarios gave way during training to dealing with nonviolent protests, securing detainees and other "less violent" tasks.

The more difficult issue would be how I could justify continuing to train Anthony to be a forward observer, to supply the platoon leader with artillery, mortars, naval gunfire, attack helicopters and other munitions. As soon as we arrived in California, I notified my immediate supervisors of my intent to apply for 1-A-O status—to be recognized as a noncombatant conscientious objector.

Surprisingly, they were not totally taken aback. Staff Sergeant

Jones and I had worked together for several months, and based on my talk about God around the water cooler, he told me, he was not entirely surprised by my decision. I never knew his first name, but Jones was *hapa*, Hawaiian for "half"; his father was white, and his mother was Asian. He had grown up in Hawaii and enlisted a few years before me. Bright, articulate and muscular, he had played football in high school, though I'm not sure what position he played. He was like Sergeant Keli'i—just slightly intimidating, but trustworthy. Someone you wanted on your side in a fight, be it physical or administrative.

In our first conversation, for some reason, Jones suggested that though I might prefer not to, I would still be expected to wear my Kevlar helmet and bulletproof vest, should my request to return to Iraq unarmed be approved. He seemed to think I had a death wish, but I felt quite differently than I did after my last deployment. I don't know why I would want to forfeit my protective gear, but even if they were taken from me, I still wanted to return with my unit.[1]

I knew that I would need to prepare my formal written request as soon as possible. Regulations require CO applicants to respond to approximately twenty-five questions, meant to outline the why, when and how of the applicant's crystallization of conscience. Once the responses are written out, the papers are submitted to one's commander—in my case Captain J. Bruce Andrews—and the process formally begins. Commanders have a limited amount of time to make progress toward resolving the request. The time period that the process should take is undefined for every branch except the Army, which specifies ninety days.[2] The last thing I wanted to do was to make my commander's job any more difficult than it needed to be (Hebrews 13:17). To receive a CO request in the middle of a training block would certainly be a burden Captain Andrews could live without. However, time was working against me.

Captain Andrews struck me as an average person trying to be known as well above average. I had this feeling that he wanted something to stand out, but nothing really ever caught my attention. His

haircut was not super sharp, his swagger about the same as any infantryman you'd find. Square jaw, weathered features and slightly dra-
matized vocal habits reflected his penchant for leading cadence
during morning runs. He had been through the arduous Ranger
Training, but in a Light Infantry unit, that was not uncommon. He
was achingly average.

He was a good leader, though, and many of the men in the company
admired him. But there was always some gray area with the forward
observers in his infantry company. When I first enlisted, FOs spent
most of their time living, eating and training with their "Red Leg"
artillery units, to whom they were also administratively accountable.
The outbreak of war necessitated a reorganization; FOs were moved
into infantry units while confusingly retaining their administrative
ties to artillery units, with whom they had decreasing interactions.
Infantry commanders rarely knew what to do with these "red-headed
stepchildren," justifying Captain Andrews's seeming disinterest.
That, or he was, in fact, simply average; as a forward observer, you got
exactly what you expected of an infantry commander, no more and
no less. His treatment of me reflected the same averageness.

The plan after our time at Ft. Irwin was to take block leave in
anticipation of our deployment. There were two blocks of leave
available to the unit, overlapping one another just slightly. I had
signed up for the second block, but the captain would be on the first
block. We would miss one another by a few days. In the meantime, I
would begin mentally preparing myself to do, for an NCO of impec-
cable standing, the unthinkable—tell the military that I could serve
violently no more, that I would have to lay down my arms in service
to Christ.

★ ★ ★

All during training, the only thing I could think about was a couple
of packages that I was expecting. The first would be coming from
Uncle Jimmy. As soon as we had touched down in California, I

emailed him to ask for a "war package," the name he gave to the items he would hand to people he met during the day for the purpose of evangelization. In each war package, he had CDs and tracts that celebrate Jesus. The stuff he handed out was not the stuff you might throw away, either. Often, he would include music from Hillsong, a popular praise band out of Australia, or the latest Rick Warren book from the Christian Inspiration section.[3]

For whatever reason, since my crystallization of conscience, I had a craving for anything and everything Christian—especially music. I had asked Jimmy to send me any Hillsong CDs he had, as well as anything else he thought a new Christian should have.

The other thing I was looking forward to in the mail was an order of books I had bought online. Before I had left, I searched "conscientious objection" on the Internet and found a (disappointingly sparse) selection of books that seemed interesting. Among them, I ordered John Howard Yoder's *What Would You Do?*[4] and a rather obscure book edited by Beth Boyle called *Words of Conscience.*[5]

I received both packages toward the conclusion of our two-week intensive training period at Ft. Irwin. My heart wouldn't stop racing. I was worried about others in my platoon seeing the packing list on the outside of the package.

To have a book with "conscience" in the title risked outing myself to others who may not be sympathetic. "Conscience" and especially "conscientious objector" are incredibly weighted terms; to utter the phrase "conscientious objector" in uniform could literally make a room go silent. COs are seen as cowards, traitors and any other derogatory phrases that you might think up. Particularly in the infantry, where courage and honor are mainstays of the culture, objection is taboo and offensive. In an atmosphere laden with imagery of fortitude, sacrifice and camaraderie, COs seem to violate nearly everything the infantryman stands for.[6]

I waited until late in the night to open my packages. The first thing I cracked was Yoder's book, exploring the classic questions posed to pacifists (e.g., "If a violent person threatened to harm a loved

one . . ."). Yoder's book is short but powerful. It is probably more accurately described as an essay than a book, since the part he wrote
was quite short. The bulk of the book is devoted to other statements
and essays on pacifism, so there is a bit of something for everybody. I
read it and was ready to move on to *Words of Conscience,* which includes official statements from various denominations on conscientious objection to war and excerpts from notables like Martin Luther
King Jr., Gandhi, A. J. Muste and the Berrigan brothers. At the very
back of the book, I stumbled upon a curious article called "The War
Prayer" that vicariously describes the emotional flurry that followed
the fall of the World Trade Center towers in 2001:

> The country was up in arms, the war was on, in every breast
> burned the holy fire of patriotism; . . . packed mass meetings
> listened, panting, to patriot oratory which stirred the deepest
> deeps of their hearts, and which they interrupted at briefest
> intervals with cyclones of applause, the tears running down
> their cheeks the while; in the churches the pastors preached
> devotion to flag and country, and invoked the God of Battles
> beseeching His aid in our good cause in outpourings of fervid
> eloquence which moved every listener.

The author was Samuel Clemens, otherwise known as Mark Twain.
He moves on to describe the particularly patriotic expressions in an
unnamed church. As a preacher begins his prayer, an aged stranger,
cloaked in pristine robes stretching all the way from his white beard
to his bare toes, makes his way silently toward the pulpit.

> With shut lids the preacher, unconscious of his presence, con-
> tinued his moving prayer, and at last finished it with the words,
> uttered in fervent appeal, "Bless our arms, grant us the victory,
> O Lord and God, Father and Protector of our land and flag!"

The stranger interrupts the passionate preacher and introduces himself
as a messenger sent from God. He has been tasked with cutting through
the fluff of the preacher's prayer so that the congregation can be sure of

what they are praying for. He reimagines the prayer:

> O Lord our God, help us tear their soldiers to bloody shreds with our shells; help us to cover their smiling fields with the pale forms of their patriot dead; help us to drown the thunder of the guns with the shrieks of their wounded, writhing in pain; help us to lay waste their humble homes with a hurricane of fire; help us to wring the hearts of their unoffending widows with unavailing grief; help us to turn them out roofless with their little children to wander unfriended in the wastes of their desolated land in rags and hunger and thirst. . . .
>
> For our sakes who adore Thee, Lord, blast their hopes, blight their lives, protract their bitter pilgrimage, make heavy their steps, water their way with their tears, stain the white snow with the blood of their wounded feet!
>
> We ask it, in the spirit of love, of Him Who is the Source of Love, and Who is the ever-faithful refuge and friend of all that are sore beset and seek His aid with humble and contrite hearts. Amen.

Is this in fact the prayer that congregation wished to send to God? Their silence at the stranger's question suggests their inability (or unwillingness) to envision the product of prayers for victory in battle. "The War Prayer" was not published until six years after Clemens's death, since, as he put it, "Only dead men can tell the truth in this world."[7] The last line of the article drives his point home: "It was believed afterward that the man was a lunatic, because there was no sense in what he said."

✷ ✷ ✷

Twain's "War Prayer" reminded me of a number of prayers uttered before airborne operations at Ft. Bragg in the chapel across from my barracks room there in North Carolina. The chaplaincy did their best to meet the expectations of liturgical traditions in some ways, and that chapel on Bastogne Ave. was one of them. There were stained glass windows, one of which I remembered in particular. At the foot of a paratrooper in Europe, reminiscent of World War II, were several townspeople, on their knees by the young man's feet. Around his helmet rested a halo, a symbol of sainthood. Was the soldier their salvation? Wasn't that dangerously close to idolatry?

There have actually been a number of soldier saints in church history; I am an avid reader of their passions.[8] But we must be careful not to venerate the figure of the soldier itself. The saints we look to in the church hold the esteem they do because of concrete actions they took to follow Jesus even when it meant they would be bumping heads with Caesar or other challenges to the lordship of Christ. Soldiering is a vocation that involves sacrifice and loyalty and camaraderie, but those virtues are distinct from the preparedness to kill. Noted pacifist Dorothy Day marveled at the martyrs, because it is they who teach us that dying for the faith, not killing for it, will save the world.

That night at Ft. Irwin, reading by flashlight in the pitch black, with my sleeping bag pulled over my head for protection, my heart burned with a holy fire—not the kind that Twain wrote about but the kind two wanderers felt on their way toward Emmaus after the crucifixion of Jesus (Luke 24:32), as their hearts burned within them while the resurrected Jesus opened the Scriptures to them and showed them how Jesus' glory was caught up in his suffering. I don't think I slept that night; I was too excited to get home and begin the Christian life.

I wondered, many years later, if that experience in the California desert was not just as Spirit-filled as the nights in Iraq I wrestled with my failure to grieve the deaths of so many Arab bodies I saw. After all, the Spirit convicts as well as renews.

★ ★ ★

I still didn't like the term "conscientious objector." It simply didn't fit how I felt called to serve.[9] By applying for 1-A-O status I was actually actively trying to return to combat. I didn't see Christians as being prohibited from being present in war, only perpetrating it. A great number of martyrs were killed trying to prevent war, and as such, in a way, they were wrapped in the overall activity of war. The Christian response to war in the first millennia was to pray for hostilities to cease—the church is always an active participant, but not in the way the world expects.

Congressional Medal of Honor recipient Desmond T. Doss, a Seventh Day Adventist who refused to carry a weapon or work on Saturdays, felt the same way, identifying himself as a "conscientious participant." Funny story: he actually did work on one Saturday—the day he earned his Medal of Honor—saving the lives of seventy-five members of his unit. When questioned about this, he reflected, "Christ healed on the Sabbath."[10] Doss also did eventually carry a weapon; later that same day he was shot in the arm, and having run out of medical supplies, he asked the soldier on his stretcher for his M-1. He emptied the cartridge of rounds and splinted his arm with the weapon. He participated in war, but did so conscientiously.

Two other conscientious objectors, Thomas Bennett and Joseph LaPointe, were also medics who refused to carry a weapon and were subsequently awarded the Medal of Honor. But the trajectory of American war fighting has been changing since World War II, when it was found that only about one quarter of soldiers on the front lines even fired their weapons. When less than 25 percent of your soldiers are shooting the enemy, the military has a problem.[11] So they changed their training.

Though my grandfather, a pilot in World War II, had been trained in weapons by firing at black and white concentric circles, the targets have gradually changed over time. My dad, who was in the Navy during Vietnam, would have fired at black or green flat cardboard silhouettes shaped like people. When I was in basic training, I shot my M-4 at plastic figures shaped and painted to resemble another human being, and recruits now are playing first person shooter games (like video games available to children) that provide immediate feedback like sounds and vibration to bring their hearts and minds closer to ending the life of another human being.[12]

It is our duty as Christians to question war.[13] The church's task, at the least, is to critically consider whether or not the centuries-old criteria for just war have been met, like there being a just cause and right intent, a clear declaration of war, noncombatant immunity, and so on.[14] Christians are not free to blindly follow orders; instead, we ultimately "obey God rather than men."[15] All too frequently we fail to engage meaningfully with how church history informs us about war. Before it was Veterans Day, November 11 was Armistice Day, commemorating the day the world thought World War I (the "War to End All Wars") had come to a close. But long before *that,* in the church calendar, November 11 was the beginning of the liturgical year and the feast day of a conscientious participant in state violence: Martin of Tours.

Martin (named after the Roman god of war) was a member of the elite Praetorian Guard, protecting the life of Caesar Julian the Apostate. At the Battle of Worms in 356 C.E., after a twenty-five-year term of military service, he told the most powerful man in the known world, "I am a soldier of Christ, it is impermissible for me to fight." When he finally did leave the Roman army, he was made a priest, despite his protests (on account of his military service). On July 4, 370, he was tricked into coming into Tours, France, to heal a peasant; upon his arrival he was acclaimed bishop, once more against his wishes.

Martin's statement to Caesar Julian was probably borrowed from Maximilian of Tebessa, one of the earliest known soldier-saints, who was beheaded in 295 at the age of twenty-one for refusing conscription on the grounds that armed service was impermissible to Christians. Martin very likely knew of Maximilian's martyrdom, as it occurred just thirty-six years before his own conscription into the same Roman Army at the age of fifteen. in 331 C.E.[16]

Soldiers of faith and conscience like Martin and Desmond have a lot to teach us about what it means to be a Christian in service to a powerful nation.[17] As I was discerning God's path in my own life, I heard a lot of opinions about what was expected of me as a Christian soldier—like "Christians are a moral force" that guides the military toward God's purposes, or that Christians must get out because military service is itself inherently evil. I tried to listen first to Jesus.

Frustratingly, Jesus does not give easy answers. Whether it is circumventing the challenge of paying taxes by pulling coins from a fish's mouth (Matthew 17:27) or failing to itemize what is owed to Caesar after we give ourselves to God (Matthew 22:21), Jesus is elusive. He never condemns centurions; he even applauds the "man under authority" who says, "Lord, I am not worthy to receive you" (Matthew 8:8-9). When Jesus applauds this humble but confident centurion, however, he does not mention his *service* but his *faith*. The man was willing to admit how short he had fallen before God—how, despite ordering others around, he didn't really have any authority to speak of next to God.

The imagery of the centurion was very helpful as I processed my experiences in Iraq and in the military in general. The church would do well to emulate the centurion's twin imperatives of humility and confidence. President Eisenhower highlighted them on his way out of office in 1961 as a warning to those who would follow him about the danger of a "military-industrial complex."[18] Reading the Bible as a centurion, as a person "under authority," Eisenhower revealed insights very different from those on either side of the question of peace who had never themselves perpetrated war. But the answers remained elusive, and I was left to navigate the threshold between God and country, between faith and service, as we made our way back from California and I was faced with the task of writing and submitting my formal request to be a noncombatant.

✫ ✫ ✫

The process of filing for CO status is complex, and for good reason. Your sincerity is on trial, and that is a hard thing to judge. If the procedure were easy, every Jane and Joe would be relying on it to get out for any number of other unscrupulous reasons. The most important questions in the packet are meant to educate an investigative officer as to the depth of your convictions.

Luckily, there are groups that help detangle the process for service personnel. The GI[19] Rights (GIR) Network offers a hotline service members can call to get free, confidential advice on matters that their command might not be inclined (or well versed enough) to be entirely upfront about, such as how to file for conscientious objection and the ramifications of going Absent Without Leave (AWOL) or taking Unauthorized Leave (UA). Most counselors are civilians without military experience, but they do a great job of explaining discharges and grievances, and are very supportive with their time and energy. I called the hotline from Ft. Irwin during our downtime, after our actual training but before we boarded planes for return to Hawaii. Calling from southern California routed me to a GIR Network cell there. I was put in touch with the group that serviced the hotline in Hawaii.

I called the number I was given for Hawaii, described my deployment and heard the voice on the other end ask me if I was sure I wanted to stay in, since it would probably be a more difficult case to make. I reassured them that it was something I felt called by God to do, that I felt called to remain in to love those with whom I was ideologically or theologically opposed. If I could serve my country nonviolently, then I did not feel it would contradict my religious beliefs. Asking explicitly to return to combat without a weapon was a long shot, but I was convinced it was where God was moving me. I knew it would make a few folks scratch their heads, having been trained to believe that freedom grew only from "the blood of patriots and tyrants."[20]

✳ ✳ ✳

One of the people I had written to during my down time at Ft. Irwin time was Shane Claiborne, whose book *The Irresistible Revolution* I had brought with me from Hawaii, along with Leo Tolstoy's *The*

Kingdom of God Is Within You (the book that inspired Gandhi's non-violence). I had ordered Boyle's *Words of Conscience* and Yoder's *What Would You Do?* Shane was the only author I was reading that was still alive at that point, and I was trying to burn time, so I figured I would write and express my gratitude for his book. My letter read in part:

> I have been reborn; slowly but surely, my old, dead skin is being shed and a new me is emerging. However, rebirth can be a painful, difficult process. . . . Over the next several weeks I will be applying for status as a Conscientious Objector. . . . God has put it on my heart to stay in and be a radical inside the military machine, if they'll have me. . . .
>
> I came to this conclusion after much study, contemplation, and most importantly, prayer. I feel there is no greater mission field than right where I am at. . . .
>
> The Lord has shown me that I can continue to love my brothers in the Army but no longer serve my former master (the sword). I believe Unconditional Love is meant for everyone, even those who partake in such practices. . . . With the Lord as my guide, I feel confident that I can continue to spread the message of peace to them, hopefully giving them a persistent, caring example of how Christians can love even those that behave in ways they steadfastly oppose.
>
> In an editorial of the *Catholic Worker,* [Dorothy Day] asks if the Martyrs did not pray that "Love would overcome Hate. That men dying for their faith, rather than killing for their faith, would save the world." I think that has become my new "war cry": to love others, even if it kills me. My life is now Christ's, to do with it as he wills. The greatest honor he could bestow on me is to give me the opportunity to give my life in order to save another.

Like others inspired by what the Spirit is doing in the church in our age, I was becoming more "radical." I always feel uncomfortable using that term, particularly as a southern California beach goer. "Radical" carries a dismissive, overly casual connotation for me, one that the more rigid culture of the military has some conflict with, to say the least. In fact, when I was in Basic Training, the first thing my Drill Sergeant sarcastically asked me, upon learning I was from California, was whether I was a "gnarly tubular dude."

But *radical* has more depth than I knew as a beach kid in SoCal. *Radical* shares its linguistic heritage with radish, a vascular plant that grows underground. To be a radical is to adhere to the deepest traditions, clinging to the ground of our faith as Christians. It was a grounding I would need as I returned to Hawaii and began the formal process to request official status as a noncombatant conscientious objector.

Serious Charges

☆

WE WERE BACK FROM Ft. Irwin, and I had not yet spoken to my company commander. I was worried because by now we had official orders to deploy. Word on the street was that we would be leaving sometime in the early fall. In that time, I hoped to complete two interviews required for the CO process (one with a chaplain to determine the depths of your sincerity, the other with a psychiatrist to determine your mental health), get a statement from my pastor at First Christian Church of Oahu, and go on leave. Needless to say, my plate would be full.

I had very little time and energy for distraction, so when Anthony asked me to his room a few days after returning from California, I was hoping for a quick meeting. I didn't get it. He seemed nervous from the start, which was unusual for our interactions. I had done my best to instill trust with him while trying to also maintain the respect requisite of our professional relationship. He stammered on uncharacteristically for a while before finally getting around to what he called me up to the barracks to ask me.

"Sergeant Mehl-Laituri, I have thought a lot about it in the last several months, after hearing about your own struggles and talking with the priest in Ft. Irwin, and I don't think I can carry a weapon as a Christian."

Anthony was worried that, as a new recruit, he would not have the credibility to apply to be a CO. He had seriously considered going AWOL.

I knew I had to choose my words carefully. I was committed to doing the right thing as a non-commissioned officer, particularly because I knew I would be coming under increased scrutiny in a few days upon submitting my own CO application. I could not allow anyone— including myself—to believe that I had facilitated his ill-advised action. But as a friend and as a Christian, I knew I needed to provide for his evolving needs, shaped as they were by trying to follow God's call in his life.

Lots of folks worry about soldiers "going CO" as a means of discharge, whose hearts aren't really in it, and it's a fair concern. However, getting a discharge (honorable or not) as a conscientious objector is by far the most difficult way out of the military. People should not apply for CO status unless they actually are fundamentally convinced, by heart or mind, of the call to nonviolence. And Anthony was.

By the time I left his barracks room, Anthony had decided to apply for discharge as a conscientious objector, status 1-O. I encouraged him not to go AWOL, as I knew it would circumvent any access to social mobility and personal stability he might otherwise enjoy should he receive an honorable discharge. Nonetheless, as I made my way back downstairs to the office, I was going over in my head places he could stay on the off-chance he felt he had no choice.

AWOL has an even more powerful stigma than CO, but in my experience, guys went AWOL all the time from Ft. Bragg. Many of them just weren't as "Hooah" as they needed to be, but not all soldiers that go AWOL are "all chewed up." In a war like Iraq, which many denominations found had failed to meet the criteria of a just war, several soldiers of conscience felt they had no choice but to go AWOL. Sometimes our submission to God looks like sedition to the world.

As Christians, we need to imagine what it might look like to take responsibility for our teachings when they come into conflict with the dictates of the state in which we hold citizenship. In China, this is the case nearly every day; the church there is accustomed (for lack of a better word) to persecution. But in many countries we have a harder time recognizing where the state ends and the church begins. It is ultimately up to the individual and his or her religious community, not the government authorities, to determine the justice of a war. When Christians are ordered to violate their sacred beliefs, the state cannot resonably expect obedience.

That's not anarchy; it's church history. Soldier saints served their country honorably up until the point at which their faith came into conflict with their service. Almost uniformly, their cadence was the same as Martin of Tours: "I am a soldier of Christ, it is impermissible for me to fight." A great number of these soldiers were martyred well into the third century—even after Roman Emperor Constantine legalized the Christian religion. Many others after that point left their posts with the blessing of their commanders and led lives of incredible regard, like Desmond Doss and other contemporary centurions.[21]

How might soldier saints and patriot pacifists form our faith, particularly in times of war? Not all Christians are pacifists, and I thank God for our diversity, but we need to prepare our congregants to respond in faith when the church finds a particular war to contradict our doctrines. Even the just war adherents among us must grapple with the charge to live our faith vigorously, to serve God first and foremost. Sometimes that puts us on the outs with the state, and we find ourselves having to lay down the sword in order to pick up our cross; sometimes laws and regulations must be subordinated to our conscience. Sometimes it means just warriors go AWOL.

Had Anthony, now a pacifist, gone AWOL, I would have helped him find sanctuary while he sorted out God's direction for his life. But in the meantime, I had my application to think about.

Anthony, with his enthusiastic determination, had his application churned out in less than a week. He had not changed his plans for leave, and would miss the company commander by a day or so, so he asked me to turn it in for him. It did not dawn on me how suspicious it would be for a non-commissioned officer and his subordinate to both turn in their packets within minutes of one another.

Once Anthony turned in his packet, I started hearing through the grapevine that I was being accused of "brainwashing soldiers." I wasn't upset. But I also wasn't stupid. If they wanted to, they could have suggested I be court martialed for sedition, which, in the military, carried the possibility of the death penalty. I didn't suspect they would court martial me for sedition, but then again, I had overlooked my own naiveté before.

Given the time crunch, the overall likelihood was failure—a court martial for refusing to draw a weapon when lawfully ordered, leading to a stripping of rank, prison time (with a federal-level conviction on my permanent record), dishonorable discharge and loss of all veterans benefits. The stakes were high, but my faith was strong.

Love and War

✫

SHORTLY AFTER SUBMITTING my packet, I was invited into my artillery lieutenant's office at Battalion Headquarters. Lieutenant Ken Violet, my Fire Support Officer, had caught word of my application and asked to speak to me. I wasn't sure what to expect, but you can't really turn down a request like that from an officer. The lieutenant was young, fresh out of ROTC, and my suspicion was that he felt he had some ground to cover with the other (infantry) officers, many of whom already had a deployment or two under their belts. Violet was an Irishman: red hair, slim, kind of short with lots of freckles. He loved to joke around with the enlisted guys, some of whom were closer in age to him than the NCOs, and it was always a pleasure to have him around; new eyes and perspective was always a breath of fresh air.

It turned out he wanted to pick my brain about how, as a Christian, I felt that I was not permitted to carry a weapon. He was a Christian himself, and he realized my convictions might have something to say about his faith. We had two conversations about war; in the first, he suggested that Jesus had already died for my sins, including the sins I might commit in combat. He also challenged me to think more fully about the Old Testament: how, if violence were forbidden, could God command the Israelites to what seemed like overt and sweeping forms of violence? I left wondering what the overall message of the Christian Bible was, if it indeed included such blatant instructions to use violence.

I looked up four words, counting how many times they appear in the Bible. What I found was encouraging, even if it was not in itself conclusive.[22] In Today's New International Version:

- The word *war* appears 133 times.

- The word *justice* appears 131 times.

- The word *peace* appears 250 times.

- The word *love* appears 584 times.

I realized how right Uncle Jimmy was the whole time. It's about love!

Meanwhile, the verses referencing war most often spoke in negative tones, in ways that named war as something bad. Over the course of about six hours that night, I wrote out my observations, cited a number of key verses and returned to Lieutenant Violet's office the next day with something like four pages of quotes from the Bible that helped me sort through what it meant to be a Christian in a time of war. There were citations from Old and New Testaments, black letters as well as red.

The second conversation did not go as well as I had hoped. I didn't know what to expect, other than to continue the conversation. I had really benefitted from his scrutiny, and I wanted to hear more about what he thought, based on the "findings" I came across the night before (copies of which I printed out for him).

I don't remember Lieutenant Violet looking at the papers I gave him as I initiated the conversation again. He did seem to quickly become agitated and resistant, but I didn't know any better than to keep poking and prodding. He may have just then realized that I had made peace with what I would do, a product of my experience on the bus in April. In any event, he seemed to shift from a mutual iron-sharpening to accusations of cowardice, scolding me for leaving soldiers like Anthony alone on the battlefield to make difficult decisions without the leadership of a Christian NCO. (I didn't mention that Anthony had already completed his CO packet; Violet probably wouldn't have taken it well.) He yelled at me to get out of his office, but then stormed out before me and slammed the door loudly, with me still inside, befuddled.

The accusation of cowardice is one that I was very aware of. Many COs are thought to be abandoning their duty out of fear of injury or death. Some applicants are in fact just trying to get out of their contract. But most enlisted personnel know that there are easier ways to get out, like failing a drug test or exploiting the (now former) "Don't Ask Don't Tell" policy.

Cowardice is such a prevalent accusation because it is easy. It doesn't require the accuser to consider that following one's conscience over and above the military culture is an uphill battle.[23] Saint Martin was accused of cowardice by his commander, Caesar Julian, for refusing to bear the sword. In response, he declared loudly,

> If it is put down to cowardice and not to faith, I will stand un-armed in front of the battle-line . . . & I will go unscathed through the enemy's columns in the name of the Lord Jesus Christ, protected by the sign of the cross instead of by helmet and shield.[24]

The vast majority of soldier saints before Martin were all martyred for refusing either to rely on violence or to obey their commander in chief over God. Sebastian, another soldier saint, was even martyred twice![25] Cowardice, while a legitimate concern, is too often a means to belittle those who otherwise insist on serving God before country. Pacifism is something that is deliberately engaged in, not the flaccid retreat of cowards and fools. Faith is a virtue, not an escape.

APPLICATION AND LEAVE

On June 5, 2006, the day after Pentecost Sunday, which commemorates the birth of the church, I finally got to see Captain Andrews and turn in my packet. The meeting was refreshingly candid and respectful. I expressed a number of times that I wanted to remain with the company and not be reassigned or discharged, that the respect, and care that I had for my unit mates was such that it prohibited me from requesting discharge. I remember being optimistically anxious, not sure what the future might hold or how things were to transpire.

He confirmed that my motives were definitely in question, but that I sounded sincere. He listened closely as I articulated what I knew to be my calling, as well as the things I was not sure about— like whether what I was being called to was a universal imperative, or whether the Spirit might indeed guide different people to different conclusions about war. I could not explain how, for whatever reason, two Christians sharing the same Scripture and tradition could come to conclusions seemingly at variance with one another. But I also made clear that ultimately they both must figure out when carrying the cross prevented them from picking up a gun, and ultimately they each had to discern when their service to our country would be subordinated to their faith in God.

In every way I knew how, I was proactive in accomplishing the tasks required of me as an applicant. I scheduled the two required interviews and printed out a copy of my application for each person in advance. Before I left his office, I supplied Captain Andrews with a copy of Army Regulation (AR) 600-43, which governs conscientious objection for the Army,[26] so that we would be on the same page as far as what was expected and required of each of us. I was trying to expedite the process so that I could deploy with my unit in the fall, when we were slotted to be back in Kirkuk, where I had deployed before with my last unit.

With my interviews scheduled and packet submitted, I went on leave the next day. I would be in California, catching up with family and then heading to the People Against Poverty and Apathy (PAPA) Festival in Maryville, Tennessee. But first, I'd be meeting Thena for dinner at her apartment in Malibu.

Thena had visited me in Bakersfield, just outside Ft. Irwin, after my training wrapped up—a wonderful thing to do, as her drive was probably longer than the couple of hours we had together. She really seemed to care for me and be committed to the idea of an "us." But during our dinner together, Thena told me that she felt we were going in different directions. I was becoming "too radical" in my faith, and it was time to part ways. It took me by surprise, especially because it was the same "radical" faith that I felt she and her family had helped awaken in me.

I had, for most of my life, considered myself a Christian. I had gone to church on and off and was relatively familiar with Scripture. I had clothes from popular "Christian" clothing companies, and I had stuck a Christian fish magnet and snarky faith-themed bumper stickers on my car. But through the experiences I was having, I became uncomfortable with those expressions of faith. They reflected a socio-commercial Christianity that had done nothing to prepare me for the gruesome and startling reality of the world around me. By speaking in terms of conversion I was implicitly but clearly calling my previous life not truly Christian, and it became a wedge between Thena and me. Sitting at a table adorned by *Not of This World* stickers and youth group logos, she exclaimed, "Maybe I don't want to give up my life. I'm comfortable as things are!"

I don't remember asking her to give up her life, but I had my doubts about a faith that dispensed cheap grace, that required nothing but store-bought statements about Jesus. Thena would go on to write a letter to my commander about our split. My faith, she reported, had "grown so rapidly . . . that our relationship could not keep up."

> I believe that Logan is being called by God to love and to serve others. Though my faith is not nearly as fervent as Logan's, I trust that God is working in his life, and I know for certain that he is ready and willing to serve his country, his fellow soldiers and also his enemies. He believes that change will not come about through more killing, but only through peace. He isn't

trying to neglect his duties—far from it. I remember him telling me in one conversation that it would be his greatest privilege to be able to give his life for another person—soldier or enemy. He is eager to serve—he yearns for it—but he wants to uphold his duty to God and serve nonviolently.

PAPA FEST

PAPA Fest was mostly made up of the type of Christians I had not previously associated with.[27] There were dreadlocks, facial tattoos, and lots of hemp clothing. From my much more rigid background, it was hard to feel comfortable at first. But over the course of the weekend, I came to find an incredibly diverse and Spirit-filled congregation of fellow Christians. They spoke of Jesus in a way I had never encountered outside church walls.

It was at PAPA Fest that I first encountered Chris Haw, a member of a community in Camden, New Jersey.[28] He and I had been in touch after he heard I was applying for noncombatant status, and we had talked on the phone a few times about serving God and country. I was looking forward to meeting him, but I didn't know what he looked like. When we first bumped into one another and realized who the other was, he grabbed me and gave me a big hug.

Even before I was in the Army, I was not much of a hugger. Either the military culture or my combat deployment had made me even less of one, but Chris didn't ask before he pulled me toward him. So I was surprised when I hugged him back and felt a startling ease. He wanted me to feel welcome, and he succeeded. That embrace set the tone for the entire rest of the weekend.

I was asked to share a bit about my decision to apply for noncombatant CO status in a seminar on Jesus and empire. For about ten minutes I talked about the situation I had just left in Honolulu: the vision on the bus in April, Anthony's application and rumors of brainwashing, and my nervousness about whether or not I would be ordered to draw a weapon. After sharing, I was prayed over by the group that was there. I am not a very charismatic person; in fact, I've been told I am stoic; so to be prayed for by the placing on of hands was a little awkward. Nonetheless, I bowed my head and opened my heart to the folks who voiced their prayers in those moments. Part of me was expecting another epiphany moment, a second awe-inspiring divine flash. But I didn't get it.

I reflected later how that was maybe just as meaningful as having my "crystallization of conscience" on the bus. I had expected, since the festival was so much more "special" than the bus, that I would *really feel the* Spirit move. When it wasn't more special, when I realized that the experience was no more moving than any other time of prayer, I found that prayer isn't so much about what you experience with your eyes and ears but the internal orientation of your heart.

Prayer is special not because of what we surround it with or the people we share it with but because it is communion with God. Communion isn't always fireworks; sometimes it can get heated, but that doesn't mean your heart always has to be on fire for your prayers to "count."

After the session, I started getting approached by a number of other festival goers about my decision to file as a noncombatant instead of requesting discharge. But the most impressing conversations I had rarely touched on my decision. One woman didn't ask questions or poke around my beliefs at all. Instead, she shared urgently about someone she cared for, a Marine torn between the cross and the sword. She broke down and told me how much the church needs the message of patriotic pacifism, how much we need to articulate an alternative to the stark binarism between faith and service.

When young people get ready to face the world as emerging adults, they want to do good; they want to serve a greater purpose. The military provides a means of fulfilling those needs: by joining the military, they are "being all they can be" and become one of "the few, the proud." If they want to fight the good fight and do so in a morally captivating way, the military provides the structure through which they can sacrifice themselves, risking themselves out of loyalty to their fellow service members.

The church doesn't do this so well. When I was in youth group, I rarely if ever thought about whether or not I would die for the person sitting next to me. But in the Army, there was no question. Even in training, there was a good chance I could get hurt; if my battle buddy failed to pass his static line off properly as we jumped from an aircraft, I would suffer the consequences. On the range, we risked injury if someone failed to eject his or her excess rounds properly. The threat and the promise of service were very real, and you witnessed it every day. But in churches, it's not always clear where loyalties lie, whether someone is willing to die for (or with) you . . .

The woman recognized the magnetism military service has for people who want to be able to know, without much doubt, that they are doing something that works toward a better world. She knew that the church had not properly prepared her loved one to express his desire to live sacrificially, that the narrative of the state had a monopoly on the language of virtue.

Over time, folks acclimated to the stiff-necked outsider with a crew cut. People stopped by my makeshift campsite instead of looking askance at the camouflage poncho stretched out over my sleeping bag and duffels. I too grew accustomed to the piercings and sharp smell of body odor, slowly learning to look at a person's heart instead of their appearance (or aroma).

People began asking me about the military, and I asked them about veggie oil and diesel engines. It was a beautiful weekend of fellowship, of having my eyes opened to the diversity of the body of Christ. These people had also given themselves over to something bigger than themselves. They found their story wrapped up in the cross as much as I did.

The most immediate question for many of them might have been more centered on poverty than violence, but we all could see our common complicity and were trying vigorously to be God's hands and feet in a broken world. They recognized problems and were striving to respond faithfully, to allow God to shape their lives and actions instead of the other way around. I began to see with my own eyes what Paul meant about the church being many parts but one body:

> There should be no division in the body, but . . . its parts should have equal concern for each other. If one part suffers, every part suffers with it; if one part is honored, every part rejoices with it. (1 Corinthians 12:25-26)

MOVEMENT FOUR

"Ours is a world of nuclear giants and ethical infants. We know more about war than we know about peace, more about killing than we know about living. We have grasped the mystery of the atom and rejected the Sermon on the Mount."

GENERAL OMAR BRADLEY, ARMISTICE DAY, NOVEMBER 11, 1948

"Lord, if your people still have need of my services, I will not avoid the toil. Your will be done. I have fought the good fight long enough. Yet if you bid me continue to hold the battle line in defense of your camp, I will never beg to be excused from failing strength. I will do the work you entrust to me. While you command, I will fight beneath your banner."

PRAYER OF ST. MARTIN, BISHOP OF TOURS UNTIL NOVEMBER 11, 397

"We must obey God rather than human beings!"

PETER, CHALLENGING STRICT ORDERS FROM THE AUTHORITIES (ACTS 5)

✯ ✯ ✯

The Good Fight

★

AT SOME POINT IN MY military service, I went to a Christian para-
phernalia store and bought myself a pair of inscribed black dog tags.
They were pretty ornate; on one side was a fancy F and underneath it
the word *fight* in all capital letters, followed by "2 TIM 4:7,8." On the
other side was a paraphrase of 2 Timothy 4:7-8:

> Fight the good fight, finish the course, keep the faith. In the
> future there is laid up for you the crown of righteousness,
> which the Lord, the righteous judge, will award to you on
> that day.

I attached it to my own chain, right next to the tags I'd been issued
when I first entered active duty. My name and Social Security number
had been slapped onto the identifying tags without my input; they
were matters of record. Also listed was my religious preference,
chosen by me but now in question.

I told the Drill Sergeant at Ft. Sill the same thing I had been telling
myself for eighteen years: "Christian, not specified." I didn't specify a
denomination because I had bounced around over my life. I was a
Christian because I was an American.

America, I thought for the most part, was fighting the good fight. We were the defenders of justice, the purveyors of democracy. Sure, violence was horrible, but sacrifices needed to be made in order to keep the peace. Evil needed to be met with superior firepower. We should not be getting ourselves into any wars of convenience, and when we did intervene, it should be with reluctance and reservation. But, to the best of my young and uninformed understanding, 9/11 was a just cause to fight a good fight.

Chaplaincy,
for Better or Worse

⭐

"So, have you been reborn?"

The question caught me off-guard. I had waited over two weeks to see John Petersen, the pastor of First Christian Church of Oahu. John was of Korean ancestry; his parents had immigrated to work the plantations (which were sugar at the time), and his father had eventually taken up ministry. John grew up surfing the north shore but never made it professionally. When that didn't work out, he took up his father's work, becoming the kind of fire-and-brimstone preacher you might imagine.

Pastor John, as he was known across the sleepy surf town of Haleiwa, loved what he did and he loved the people he did it with. Though the church we met at was small, there would be two services, each packed all the way to the slat windows. I absolutely loved the music the worship band played, but I don't remember being much excited about his preaching. Come to think of it, I never heard him give a sermon that wasn't based on the book of Revelation.

On my lap rested a stack of papers that made up my application to be a conscientious objector, part of which required information about the pastor or leader of my religious community. I had been attending NSCF for a few months by this point, and I had been put in touch with Pastor John directly by his secretary after letting him know of the situation with my CO application.

There are lots of ways to start a conversation. Maybe start off with something light, like "How are you?" or "How was the drive?" Instead, John seemed to be asking me whose team I was on. If my answer was no, would we have to reschedule?

"Yeah, I think so," I replied. John asked me a few questions about my history, including how long I had been attending NSCF, but our conversation never went beyond logistical details.

Weeks later, after church one Sunday, I approached him after most of the congregation had dispersed to catch up with him about the packet. I was hoping he'd engage the particulars of my request, like whether he felt returning to war as a noncombatant made any sense theologically. But John seemed focused on my rejection of just war traditions. He mentioned Pearl Harbor (which everyone on Oahu has a strong connection to), but nothing of much substance, I felt. In an email later, his deeper thoughts came out:

> OK, so you've become a Pacifist. You would rather let an evil enemy kill you, as well as the innocent American women, mothers and babies you—as an Army Soldier—swore to defend and protect, than to kill the same evil enemy. Now, to be fair, you will argue "That's not what I said!" but it is the only logical end to your Pacifist ways. If every soldier in the US Army lays down their weapons, we in effect surrender the USA to the militant Muslims.

Tragically, his response did not surprise me. One night during a gathering at his home in Haleiwa, I noticed a placard in his kitchen that read something like "Strengthen my heart, O Lord, that others might know me by my love, but hobble my enemy's feet, that I might know him by his limp."

✯ ✯ ✯

I had chatted with a chaplain during training at Ft. Irwin, and our meeting, while not as troubling as my interaction with Pastor John, had similarly put me on guard. That chaplain had remarked that my requesting status as a noncombatant CO was, in effect, turning my back on the military. He casually suggested I would forfeit my benefits through the Veterans Administration, such as my GI Bill and access to healthcare, even though my discharge might be honorable.

He wasn't necessarily correct. The discharge classification is downgraded only by courts martial; but CO status doesn't automatically result in dishonorable discharge. The problem comes in the time between applying for CO status and when it is officially granted. Often applicants are faced with an order they cannot obey in good faith and conscience—for example, being ordered to conduct weapons training. A disobeyed command subjects the person to judicial process, which puts the CO application on hold, if it is not abandoned entirely. Sometimes an applicant is discharged for reasons having nothing to do with their status, effectively voiding their application; that's one reason there are so few applications recorded.[1] Honorably discharged soldiers, regardless of their CO status, retain all benefits that accrue to veterans. I didn't know that at the time, so I was inclined to believe the chaplain, but my resolve was such that I was prepared for the worst, including time in the brig. A friend of mine says "There is no greater freedom than the freedom to follow your conscience"; I might be put in chains, but my conscience would be clear and free.[2]

I had kept a running conversation going with my own unit chaplain, a Presbyterian minister, since my crystallization of conscience on the bus. We had a few informative conversations before things began to sour within the company itself. During one meeting he told me that he admired my fortitude, but that I shouldn't worry about the outcome. Whether the packet was approved or not was God's plan. It was a beautiful reminder to let the chips fall as they may and trust in God, but I had reason to believe that my unit was not acting in good faith. How did his advice speak to the reality of human moral frailty? What if my unit was, even inadvertently, working against (what might be) God's plan of me serving nonviolently?

When it came time to meet the requirements of my formal request, my unit chaplain suggested that for him to conduct the interview might compromise our counselor/counselee relationship. I could not have been more grateful for his observation, as I think he was right. I ended up meeting with another unit's chaplain, not far from where my own unit was located. Above the door to his office sat an engraving of the motto of the Chaplain's Corps: PRO DEO ET PATRIA, "For God and Country." Next to the door was a table, adorned with, among other things, the prayer of St. Francis: "Make me an instrument of your peace." I felt like Alice on the precipice of the rabbit hole: curiouser and curiouser . . .[3]

The military does not "do" peace, the chaplain's prayer of St. Francis notwithstanding. The military does war. And it should; that is what it is trained for and best equipped to carry out. But the core of the Army is the armed infantry—everything else is, literally, "combat support"—so how can we hope to be an instrument of peace when everywhere we go in the execution of our vocation requires that we carry a firearm? The prayer seemed ill-placed at best, but I was at least willing to entertain the idea.

I half-expected the chaplain to be antagonistic. Instead, he quickly assured me that, while he expected us to "respectfully disagree," his job was not to criticize but to discern my level of sincerity. I was immediately put at ease. I've found that respect has that effect on people.

We talked for nearly an hour. Recognizing the urgency of my request, the chaplain promised to write up his recommendation for me in under a week. I was as relieved by his manner as I was with his final recommendation, which read in part:

This decision he has been struggling with has come at a high price for him, but because he feels so strongly he is now more resolved to follow through. [Sergeant] Mehl-Laituri is articulate in his views, and it is obvious that he has done a lot of research and contemplation concerning Conscientious Objector status. As the interviewing Chaplain, I feel that he has a depth of sincerity in his beliefs.

On Guard

☆

THE WORD ON THE GRAPEVINE back at the unit during my leave was that my artillery officer, Lieutenant Violet, had been belittling me in front of some of the lower enlisted personnel. He was not happy about my decision to apply as a noncombatant (much less so about my having "brainwashed" Anthony into submitting his own request), perhaps harboring a chip on his shoulder after our conversations about war and peace. Some of the comments supposedly included physical threats.

Enlisted Army personnel, upon becoming non-commissioned officers (at the rank of E-5, or "sergeant"), become the "backbone of the Army." There is a deep respect between NCOs and officers, and the relationship is built upon a solid foundation of trust. When that trust is compromised, the cohesiveness of the unit can break down in a heartbeat. For that reason, there is a strict and explicit prohibition on talking down an NCO or officer in front of "Joes" (those of rank E-4 and below). To do so undermines the authority of the NCO and officer corps.

There is a kind of class distinction, incidentally, between officers and enlisted personnel. Enlisted are by and large less educated, younger and often from harsher economic backgrounds. This is partly explained by the incredible amount of money devoted to military recruitment and enlistment. Enlisted personnel do their service before gaining higher education. Officers, by contrast, only enter the service after gaining at least a bachelor's degree. The cultural divide between enlisted and commissioned needs to be acknowledged, but there is also an "economic draft" at play. In over six years in the Army, I heard maybe a handful of stories about joining for patriotic reasons (all of them post-9/11). More often, people like myself had enlisted for financial reasons. The majority of recruits come from urban and rural areas. A nonprofit in 2008 compared unreleased recruitment numbers with census data and found that the highest rates of enlistment in New York City indisputably coincided with areas with the highest high school dropout rates.[3]

When I alerted my supervisors about being undercut by Lieutenant Violet, Staff Sergeant Jones didn't take much action. To make matters worse, I found that my unit had not made any effort to assign an investigative officer to my CO claim. Two weeks was plenty of time to find a captain to collect the files and letters I was accumulating for the informal hearing that I hoped to have before our deployment. But nothing had been done, apparently, and now time was running out quickly.

By this time, I started to get pretty nervous. I felt the hostility beginning to be more open. Looking back, I could have been more patient, but I was trying to make doubly sure that my claim would be processed in the States. I knew that if it were delayed until we got to Iraq, I would not be able to call witnesses and write a rebuttal if necessary.

I was starting to wonder whether my unit really intended to process my claim or was simply opting to let circumstances dictate things. If our deployment date came before my claim was processed, I might be ordered to draw my weapon even though I had made it clear that, as a Christian, I would never again touch a firearm. I would then refuse a direct order and likely be court martialed for exercising my conscience.

This scenario had always been in the back of my mind as a possibility. Now, as I realized that my unit had taken no discernable action in two weeks, the possible was beginning to look likely. I had no qualms with jail time—a great number of saints have been put behind bars for refusing to obey laws and lawful orders their consciences opposed. But I also didn't see any reason in acquiescing to something that seemed patently unjust. Finding an officer to serve as an investigative officer to process my application didn't seem like too much to expect.

I realized that nobody was going look out for my interests but me. I knew that the American Civil Liberties Union took cases for free if they were compelling, so I researched the local ACLU chapter and found out how to request support. I knew of a case in New York not long before of another CO applicant, Corey Martin, who secured a federal injunction to keep him stateside until his process was complete. I figured the same course of action would help ensure I received the due process afforded me as a citizen of the United States.[4] On June 20, two weeks after submitting my packet and almost two months after making clear to my unit my intent to file, I wrote to the ACLU and asked for their support. I printed out the letter, put it in the mail and hoped for the best.

MENTAL STATUS EVALUATION

The same week I met with the chaplain, I arranged for an appointment with a psychiatrist working on base at the Soldier Assistance Center to conduct the required Mental Status Evaluation (MSE). As best I can tell, the purpose of the psychiatrist in the CO process is to ensure that the service member has the mental coherency not only to go through the process but to have reliably applied in the first place. A psychiatrist can effectively override the CO request by recommending a medical discharge. Whereas the chaplain judges sincerity, the psychiatrist judges, well, sanity.

Civilians staff the mental health department at Schofield Barracks. I appreciated that; having a civilian as my evaluator seemed to avoid any question of partiality. I made sure to drop off a copy of the statement I had turned in to Captain Andrews so that I didn't have to repeat myself any more than absolutely necessary. Dr. Leonard, my caseworker, was a great listener. I know because he didn't do a whole lot of talking, which was fine with me because he reminded me of Marlon Brando in his later years. The doctor was heavyset, his voice was deep and his words slightly slurred. We met in the afternoon, and the light coming in from a nearby window revealed a thin layer of sweat on his forehead. I couldn't take my eyes from it when I glanced in his direction, so I spoke mostly with my eyes wandering around his small office.

I explained to Dr. Leonard that, as a result of a vision I saw on my way to train in the desert of California, I was seeking 1-A-O status so that I could deploy to contested territory in northern Iraq (unarmed) with my infantry company. After I had regurgitated all the particularities and done my best to put some reason behind it all ("radical" faith doesn't really fit well into clinical settings, I've found), he remarked that I was perhaps the most mentally stable person he had met with in years. Ultimately, he was very sympathetic to my situation and wanted to help in whatever way he could.

Lieutenant Violet had made a comment in our earliest conversation that I hadn't understood at first. He claimed that there was no way the unit could deploy an unarmed soldier. It was a political landmine; if I got hurt, the Army would have a public relations nightmare on their hands. I thought he was joking or something. But I wanted to return to Iraq because of my crystallization of conscience. The certainty I had in my call to return to Iraq was deeper than they seemed willing to imagine. I was ready to die because I had discovered something to live for: love for God and neighbor, love for my country, but also for my enemies.

Dr. Leonard may have understood that I wanted to go back, but he also knew that doing so could be interpreted as a sign of mental illness. He carried the responsibility to attend to the inherent dangers in sending an unarmed soldier to war. He had to discern how to best perform his professional obligation, which could have meant to protect me from harm (by insisting I be made non-deployable) or to aide me in my cause (by verifying my good mental health). I left his office satisfied that he would do what he thought to be best.

I got his report a couple of weeks later, the first week in July.

This [adjustment] disorder is of sufficient severity that [service member] is not expected to remain fit for duty in the Army. . . . Patient is not deployable. He cannot carry a weapon. He is reporting that he is a Conscientious Objector and objects to war.

The competitive part of me got defensive. What part of "fit" did I not meet? I was disappointed in his recommendation that I be made non-deployable, since I made it explicitly clear that I was trying to deploy, that physically and mentally, I could not have been better prepared. But, at the same time, I knew that my behavior could indeed be quite difficult to interpret. I had mixed emotions, to say the least.

✳ ✳ ✳

Before my break up with Thena, I had gotten close with her brother, Nathan, a nondenominational campus minister at a community college in the heart of Honolulu. He was short and round without being flabby, had his father's dark hair and large brown eyes, a trusting face, and a gentle voice. Whenever I ordered a stout at the Irish pub downtown, I would think of him.

As a minister on campus, I assumed he had theological training, and we would often talk about the church and current events. His beliefs were more conservative than mine, and our interactions would always be a reminder that enriching dialogue is not only possible but essential. I suspected he felt differently about war than I did, but I never deliberately broached the subject of war and peace with him. He knew about my application, but it didn't seem to faze him, and his relative emotional distance was a welcome respite from the relational maelstrom that swirled around me.

Not long after the trip to Ft. Irwin, I began thinking about baptism. I didn't know much about church practices, but I knew enough to know that baptism was one of the sacraments expected of all believers. At some point, I called to ask my mom if she had ever had me baptized when I was young. I figured there was a chance she had. She took some time to think about it, but she ended up pretty sure that I had not been baptized.

I didn't have a good idea what purpose a baptism would serve other than as a public witness to my new faith in Jesus Christ. Nonetheless, I mentioned my interest to Nathan. He had a barbeque planned for the Tuesday immediately following my return to Hawaii from PAPA Fest, and he wondered if I would be interested in getting baptized then. I vaguely remember suggesting it might be doable, as long as I didn't have a duty to pull that night for my battalion. On Monday, the day before the barbecue, I learned I'd be off duty, so I phoned Nathan to RSVP.

I don't remember thinking much about it at all after that. I had heard back from the ACLU, indicating their interest in my case. I was set to meet with two lawyers that coming Friday, July 7. It didn't occur to me that Tuesday, the day I might be baptized, was July 4.

I didn't know the people from Nathan's campus ministry group all that well, but I will do just about anything for access to a jacuzzi, which his apartment complex sported. We had a great panorama of Waikiki from the pool deck some five floors up. The night was typical for Hawaii: warm, breezy, star-filled and beautiful. We played tennis, ate burgers and swam in the pool while we waited for the fireworks to ignite above Ala Moana Harbor.

We watched for what must have been at least thirty full minutes as the fiery pageant danced across the twilight's last gleaming. As the bombs' bright bursts faded and the last rockets glared red, we simmered down, hanging around lazily in the ambient glow of the pool lamp.

It was only a matter of time before I would make my way back to my car and drive home, across the island, to the North Shore, where my fate lay still undetermined. In the meantime I made my way to the jacuzzi to forget all my worries—all the lawful orders, legal concerns and officer drama. I closed my eyes and took a number of deep breaths.

Then someone tapped me on the shoulder. "You ready?" Nathan inquired above me.

"For what?"

"You said you wanted to get baptized tonight," he reminded me gently. "People are waiting."

I blinked myself back to coherency, trying to remember when I had said I "wanted" to get baptized on the Fourth of July. Could I tell him I needed to get home to wash my hair? Would that be too obvious?

"OK, gimme a second?"

"Yeah, sure. We're over there when you're ready, on the other side of the pool."

Nobody had left; literally every person was still there, gathering around a couple of picnic tables, looking doubtfully in my direction, wondering why I was off lounging in the spa. I dipped below the warm water for privacy. Surfacing, acutely aware of the significance of the moment I faced, I prayed as quickly as I could manage:

> God, make my life a living sacrifice. Help me to never shy away from steadfast service in the good fight of the faith. Create in me a new heart, make me a new being, help me to remain in the battle without avoiding hardship. Where you lead, I will follow. May I glorify you in every breath of my lungs, every beat of my heart, and every word of my mouth. Amen.

I took a deep breath and moved toward the crowd of witnesses.

Baptism and Rebirth

⭐

THE ANSWER TO THE QUESTION of whether man is good has evaded humanity from the beginning of the world. The best I have come up with is conscience. War showed me how pitiful and wretched people could be, but I also witnessed the trust made possible through martial camaraderie. We are capable of audacious acts of virtue and the most horrifying acts of evil, of both charity and callousness. God created us free—free to hurt one another and free to help one another. It is up to us to choose, but we are to choose the good.

As I approached the crowd waiting for my baptism, I knew I would have to explain my conscience and why it was part and parcel to my walk with God. This new community I was entering, which fancied itself the body of Jesus, the Son of God, would hold me accountable to the good I would need to discern and choose every day for the rest of my life.

My baptism would be the first day of the rest of that life—a new life lived sacrificially, but a deeper sacrifice than when I donned the uniform of a soldier. If I was to take up my cross, it meant I would have to lay down my sword. Like Cain, I had a second chance to master the sin that crouches constantly at my door; I could reject the easy path of retribution and embrace the hard, redemptive Way of Jesus. By being baptized, I was articulating that intent publicly, so that I could be aided in my effort and held accountable when I failed.

In his book *What's Wrong with the World,* British writer G. K. Chesterton wrote, "The Christian ideal has not been tried and found wanting. It has been found difficult; and left untried."[5] I had stumbled upon the love that birthed the universe, the love that has fueled creation from beginning and will until the end. There was literally no going back. If I had tried, I would have lived the rest of my life in the knowledge that I had refused my vocation, that I had left the difficult path untried. Christ beckoned, and I had no choice but to respond.

★ ★ ★

I never thought explicitly about taking my own life, but it is clear to me that I didn't have a sincere interest to live. In the midst of suicide bombers and terrorism, as I was thinking about what it meant to be a Christian, with its long history of martyrdom, I struggled to understand the difference between a suicide bomber and a Christian martyr. The language of baptism, after all, is laden with words about death. Being "reborn" assumes that one is rising from death. Death, it seems, is requisite to new life. But in adopting this mantle of new life, Christians recognize that their life is no longer theirs, but belongs to God. Our lives are living sacrifices; not our own will, but God's, be done (Luke 22:42). We let it be with us according to God's desire (Luke 1:38). My movement toward baptism was not unlike my preparation for deployment; I was embracing death in each, but in very different ways.

The distinction between a suicide bomber and a Christian martyr, I decided, was twofold. First, suicide bombers insist on being in control, whereas Christian martyrdom involves the relinquishment of control. Second, the martyr recognizes that God is the owner of each life, including both the life of the martyr and the life of their attacker. Heschel calls life "not our own property, but a possession of God. And it is this divine ownership that makes life a sacred thing."[6]

Suicide bombers claim ownership of their lives and take ownership of the deaths they cause; the true martyr in contrast relinquishes control of their own life and surrenders the life of their attacker to God, who declares, "It is mine to avenge; I will repay" (Romans 12:19). Recognizing God's sovereignty in the face of your own murderer is perhaps the greatest test of faith. The martyr understands that life is not in and of itself what has value, but God's ownership of that life—regardless of religion, race or nationality.

Being baptized was, for me, not so much a grasp at control and suicide but an embrace of self-denying martyrdom. I was welcoming the death of myself in favor of being revived by and in Christ.

✷ ✷ ✷

Nathan and his friend Harland would be performing the baptism. They wore white shrouds as they waded into the pool before me, inviting me into the water with them. The image of each of them looking up at me, waiting for my decisive step into the pool, will be with me forever. I could have chosen to stay mostly dry by being sprinkled. I'm glad I didn't.

I had no idea what to expect. Harland prayed over me as he and Nathan each had one hand on my back and the other holding an arm; "God, please accept Logan as a follower of your Son, Jesus Christ." I looked at Nathan as he uttered those timeless words:

> I baptize you in the name of the Father, the Son and the Holy Spirit.

With that, I was gently lowered backward into the water. Nathan knew I surfed, that he could trust me to hold my own breath and not get water in my nose. It felt like I was underwater forever, but it surely was only for a split second: eyes closed, I was bathed in the warmth of the company of brothers in Christ. The radiance of the pool lamp, breaking through my eyelids, evoked the light of Jesus, illuminating our journey of faith.

I felt Nathan and Harland urge me back to the surface, which rushed to meet me too soon. I wished I could stay in the pool forever. As I broke into the balmy Honolulu air, the water cascaded off my face and poured out of my ears. I could hear the clapping of the crowd. As the final droplets fell from my eyes, the clapping mixed with the sound of a handful of fireworks, set off long after the end of the official demonstration. They were baffling and beautiful in their timing; the heavens seemed to be rejoicing. My ears rang and my heart sang with each pyrotechnic burst.

About a year prior, the burst of light and noise would have made my heart stop and my ears stand on edge. These were the sights and sounds of war, and the invasive instinct of "fight or flight" would have gouged its way into my mind. But God was doing a new thing in my life. With fire and water, my baptism was sacramentally paralleling the failed rescue attempt in northern Iraq. There I had fought back the frigid scepter of death in the midst of the wilderness with my combat battle buddies. Here I found new and everlasting life bathed in the warm light of living water with a new band of brothers. Before, I had been dragged from the dark waters, numb, cold and surrounded by death. Now I was being lifted by a new community, warm, alive and covered in light. The old things were being made new; life was bursting forth through, and despite, death.

Coming to the Wire

☆

THE WRITING ON THE WALL in my unit was becoming clearer to me by the day; my CO status would be an uphill battle, and I'd be alone in the fight. I had learned that if I needed something done, I would have to make sure it happened myself. Writing the ACLU was essentially my last-ditch effort. Without some kind of intervention, there was a good chance that there would be no hearing, no commander recommendation and no due process to speak of, by the time of my next deployment.

The only question on my mind was whether they would order me to violate my conscience in Hawaii or in Iraq. The penalty would be steeper if they waited until Iraq. I had no problem with prison time, but if I could avoid it, I intended to. Being a pacifist doesn't mean I'm stupid.

The Friday after my baptism was the day I had scheduled to meet with the local ACLU chapter and another lawyer, Greg Benjamin. Greg was a southerner he reminded me of Foghorn Leghorn, but I had no idea how he came to be in Hawaii. His lips smacked when he talked; he pursed them out for effect at times, though I don't know if it was intentional. His matter-of-fact nature didn't do anything to console me in what I was sure would be the beginning of the end.

I met with Greg and a representative of the ACLU on Friday afternoon. By that time, I had a pretty good idea that my unit would be deploying within a month. It was coming down to the wire, and my chances of deploying without incident were waning fast.

Greg was an independent lawyer, but with the collaboration with the ACLU (originally founded as the American Union Against Militarism), his work would be done pro bono. The only option I seemed to have was Corey Martin's path: to prepare to file for an injunction in order to make sure my process was handled stateside, before deploying. There is a lot of talk about abridgment of rights upon enlistment—such as the right to bad-mouth the commander in chief—but those secured by the Constitution, such as the right to due process, never go away. Nevertheless, due process is easier to protect while stateside than while on the front lines.

When I sat down with Greg and the ACLU counsel, I was convinced we were in the advanced stages of catastrophe. To my surprise, the lawyers did not share my anxiety. They reassured me that a month was "plenty of time." I explained the process of my case to date and gave him copies of the additional evidence I would submit at the hearing, mostly letters witnessing to my sincerity, including the one written by Thena shortly after our breakup.

One of Greg's first questions was about my beliefs: was my objection political? Did I object to this war, or all wars? As a lawyer, he was aware that my chances were slim to none if I were a selective objector. Selective conscientious objection (SCO) is objection not to "war in any form" but particular conflicts that violate one's religious or moral training and belief.

The just war doctrine, inasmuch as it is left to "the prudential judgment of those who have responsibility for the common good"[7] (including individual service members), is equivalent to selective objection. Pacifism, which I had claimed for myself, is recognized legally as universal objection to "war in any form," but laws do not protect objection to a particular war that fails to meet just war criteria.[8] He just wanted to get a feel for the legal ramifications of my claim, but on paper I was fine—I was a "true" pacifist, one that military regulations recognized as legitimately objecting to all war.

"OK, so who is your investigative officer?" Greg asked.

"I have no way of knowing. I'm not sure if one has been assigned yet."

"It's been over a month, and you don't have an IO?"

"Not to my knowledge."

He picked up his phone and dialed a number from memory. I heard only his side of the conversation.

Hi, is this the 25th Infantry Division legal section? My name is Greg Benjamin, I practice law in Honolulu, and I have a client in my office that has submitted a request to be recognized as a conscientious objector. He filed on June 5th, and I'm hoping to be sent a copy of his request packet.

That was it? His first act was to ask for a copy of the packet I just handed him? I began to realize why lawyers get such a bad rap.

Greg turned his attention to me and sighed. "Well, now we wait!"

At least I'll get some good reading done in the brig, I thought as I shuffled out of his office.

Reporting for Duty

☆

MONDAY MORNING, JULY 10, was a morning like any other, except that it was the week after my baptism, the sixth day after my entrance into the body of Christ, the church. I woke up, grabbed a glass of water, put on my PT uniform and stumbled to my car. Rolling into the unit area, I saw Staff Sergeant Jones pacing outside, obviously waiting for something. That something turned out to be me. Pacing wasn't really his thing; something was afoot.

"First Sergeant Hartman wants you in his office *right now*, Sergeant Mehl-Laituri."

First Sergeant Hartman was "old school" Army. He had enlisted when they still beat up recruits, before the military "softened." His features were taut, like he pulled his face on too tight and couldn't quite open his eyes all the way. It wasn't even seven in the morning and he had a five o'clock shadow. His body was top-heavy, like Buzz Lightyear's stubbier, more sinister doppelganger.

With a dutiful "Roger," I proceeded directly for First Sergeant Hartman's office. Mornings before PT are usually a time dedicated for a "leaders huddle" to discuss the day's priorities, so the whole enlisted leadership team was in the office as I stepped before First Sergeant Hartman's desk and assumed the position of "parade rest": hands clasped rigidly behind my back, eyes straight forward, feet planted exactly shoulder width apart. "First Sergeant, Sergeant Mehl-Laituri, reporting as requested."

The platoon sergeants and staff sergeants were all awkwardly silent. Some avoided looking at me; others peered out from behind hands that rubbed their temples or massaged faces. I felt like a spectacle; they all seemed to be there to witness, to share in, my final fall from favor.

"Well, Sergeant Mehl-Laituri, you got what you wanted."

As soon as he said it, I knew two things:

A. He did not know what I wanted (or he didn't believe that what I told him I wanted was actually what I wanted).

B. I would not be deploying with my unit to Iraq.

My shoulders fell; my crisp stance slumped. I'm pretty sure he saw it. I'm pretty sure he didn't care.

"We got your little letter from the lawyer over the weekend."

I didn't know about any letter, or why it might be smaller than any other letter. I was too nervous to allow myself to laugh at the image of a snack-sized letter being delivered to the battalion office.

"You've forced my hand, Sergeant Mehl-Laituri. I have no choice but to reassign you to rear detachment."

I could only guess what had happened. I speculated that the phone call on Friday afternoon triggered a chain reaction at the division level, above Hartman's head, that would have required time and energy unavailable with so little time before our deployment. Rear detachment (Rear-D) is the part of a unit that remains in the States to administer affairs for the forward deployed soldiers, a job nobody wants. It was made very clear to me by First Sergeant Hartman that my reassignment was for medical reasons, since my MSE evaluator had recommended I be made non-deployable. However, in the Army, those decisions are always at the commander's discretion. If he had wanted to, Captain Andrews could have easily tossed my MSE in the trash.[9] There was a choice, despite First Sergeant Hartman's objections to the contrary; I could still be deployed, but now I knew I wouldn't be.

In the First Sergeant's office that morning, I watched my prospects for deploying with my comrades slip away from me. If it were funny, I would call it a comedy of errors, but I wasn't laughing.

CHANGE OF COMMAND

In a military unit, commanders change relatively frequently. The change of command ceremony is highly liturgical; it's a script that is supposed to instill meaning and purpose into what would otherwise just be an administrative task.

The ceremony is consummated by passing the unit flag, called a guidon, from the old commander to the new. There is much ado about taking the guidon from the hands of the standing commander, placing it in the hands of the incoming commanding officer, and the symbolic release of authority from one to the other. The most symbolically significant act is the pregnant pause when both commanders have their hands on the guidon. The eagerness of the new commander exists in precise proportion with the reluctance of the old.

The week between my baptism and my eviction from my infantry company was like that pregnant pause. My new commander had placed his hands on my life even as my former commanders were maintaining an anxious grip. I was waiting for the world to release me, to allow me the same honor as St. George before me, to "leave all in order to serve the God of Heaven."[10] The change of command that I was undergoing is what the church knows as *metanoia*: repentance, a total life reorientation that is not just symbolic but embodied and enacted.

★ ★ ★

In the days immediately following my departure from my infantry company, I went through the normal paperwork to "out-process" a unit. The most memorable moment was when I turned in my weapons card, the slip of paper you keep with you and exchange for your rifle when you have to clean it, prepare for training or go to war. Something inside me hinted that turning in my card was a means of worship, the closest I would come to laying down my weapon in recognition of the age-old cadence of soldier-saints: "I am a soldier of Christ; it is impermissible for me to fight." I had reached the limits of my service to country; it was time now to serve God.

On Thursday Staff Sergeant Jones told me that Captain Andrews wanted to see me in his office. I had already cleared the company, so being called back was a little strange. It made me nervous; what on earth could he need to tell me that one of the NCOs couldn't relay for him?

Weeks earlier, I had asked to see him about my lieutenant's derogatory remarks about me to lower enlisted personnel. Protocol called for me, the subordinate, to bring the matter to the captain as the next ranking officer over both of us. My request for a meeting had been denied, by either circumstance or design.

I suspected that, to square away all the loose ends in regards to my departure from the company, Captain Andrews needed to acknowledge my request on some administrative level. That was my best guess, and it was partly correct. The Uniform Code of Military Justice protects people's access to their commander; if there is an issue with a mid-level leader and utilizing the regular chain of command is not appropriate, or if a problem is not being resolved in the manner it should be, even a private is guaranteed an audience with their commanding officer. It is called "Open Door Policy" despite usually taking place behind closed doors. Kind of ironic, but that's another issue.

Shortly after first formation that Thursday, I walked into Captain Andrews's office, knocked on his door and waited for his invitation before entering. He had some notes on his desk. It seemed like he had been expecting me.

He asked me what I wanted to see him about, which threw me off guard. Upon being reassigned, I didn't think Open Door had any relevance any longer. Hadn't I been told to report to him? I replied that the issues that I had raised had been more or less resolved by First Sergeant Hartman, either by the fact of my reassignment or by insisting that there was nothing that could be done.

I had received the chaplain's and psychiatrist's reports the week prior, just before seeing the lawyers in Honolulu. Standard practice was that the unit commander was forwarded copies separately, before they were sent to the service member, but Captain Andrews seemed to be reading them for the first time. He seemed surprised at what he had read, particularly the Mental Status Evaluation, where Dr. Leonard had written that I "was" a conscientious objector. Captain Andrews felt that I had lied to the psychiatrist in order to expedite my departure from the military. "You have grasped at every f***ing straw that you can to get out of this deployment," he told me.

"I don't believe you're a conscientious objector at all. I don't believe any of this religion . . . this conversion nonsense at all. I believe that you think you've hit on the perfect scheme to get out of a deployment because no one can prove that you're not a conscientious objector. The reason that you're getting out of it is because you're not worth keeping. It would be wrong to say that you are useless to this company. Useless would imply that you have zero utility. You have negative utility; you have used up the time and the energy and the effort of this chain of command to an extraordinary degree—more than any four or five other people in this company put together. Your conduct is not becoming of a non-commissioned officer. The fact that I have to look at you with E-5 rank on is disgusting. You are not worthy of it. You're not worthy of going to Iraq with us. I cannot f***ing trust you. That's why the colonel and I made the decision to just get rid of you as fast as we possibly can. There is no utility in keeping you.

"You should take a few minutes to sit down and think about who your actions help, because I can think of two f***ing groups: yourself, personally, and the enemies of America. And that's it. I don't want to see you in my infantry company ever again; I am giving you a direct order to never set foot on Alpha Company again. Do you understand this?"

"Roger, sir," I responded.

"All right. Get out."

Captain Andrews had misinterpreted the mental status evaluation in a key way: my request for CO status was not an application but a declaration of the truth about who I am. I was a conscientious objector regardless of what the Army wanted to call me. After all, the founders didn't write a "request for independence" from Great Britain; they crafted a "Declaration of Independence" based on a new reality at which they had arrived.

Naming a person has incredible power. It's why in preparation for their confirmation of faith, catechumens take another name. It's why African people subjected to slavery in American history often would not refer to themselves by the name written on their bill of sale. It's why I felt more connection to the fellow armed service folk I interacted with when we referred to one another not by our nametape on our uniform but by our first names. They are my siblings not by merit of the martial fraternity we share, by the trials of boot camp or our crisp uniforms, but by our rebirth into the body of Christ. "Family" takes on a whole new meaning upon baptism.

If the Army refused to acknowledge the truth about me, and I landed in jail thanks to my declaration of conscientious objection, that would not change who I was. My identity is internally dictated; it comes from my heart, where God has written a higher law.

Lost in Paradise

☆

HAWAII IS OFTEN CALLED PARADISE, and it isn't difficult to tell why. The word *paradise* comes from a word that means "gardens." But for me, Oahu was like paradise not because of its gardens but because of the waves. Going surfing was my escape, my return to normalcy. Alone on the water, I could be at peace. The tears that would sometimes tumble clumsily down my cheeks seemed to be hurrying back to the comfortable familiarity they had with the saline sea in which I so often found rest.

During the summer of my CO application, I wasn't able to get to the beach very often. But I treasured the time I had to surf. In the evenings, I would watch as pinks and purples and yellows danced on the surface of the tropical water. I'd lose track of time thinking out loud about my situation and talking to God in between wave sets. It was as close to heaven as I think I might get on this side of death.

My time in the water became centrally important to me in the final weeks of the whole ordeal, as I watched relationships crumble and my reputation dissolve. I felt the cost of discipleship in a way I wasn't expecting. Many of my civilian friends grew distant, not returning phone calls or arranging surf sessions. Friends of mine in the battalion knew only that I was not conducting weapons training and was in some kind of tiff with my lieutenant, who was likely venting his disappointment to others. Everybody was busy, and we were not able to keep in touch. I had also been discouraged by my unit command from speaking about my CO application (supposedly to protect my privacy). The circle of friends in which I could confide was shrinking, and the voices of opposition were growing.

My carefully groomed reputation as a forward observer had crumbled. Prior to my CO request, my Non-Commissioned Officer Evaluation Report (NCOER) had read "Stands up for what he thinks is right" and "Promote ahead of peers." It had been changed to read "Forces his personal opinions on his soldier," "Complains excessively," and "Refuses to adhere to Army Regulation procedures for personnel actions."

Anthony had been reassigned to another company for the stated purpose of keeping him from my "brainwashing." He then withdrew his own CO request, inadvertently strengthening the claims being made against my character. As far as I could tell, by living out my faith I had literally lost every friend I had.

Somewhere in there, I squeezed in some reading. I can't remember how I stumbled across it, but I became intrigued by *Paradise Lost*, an epic poem written by John Milton in the seventeenth century. He had hoped his prose would help secure the English language's place among the classic romance tongues. When I didn't have anything else to do, I would open it up and strengthen my vocabulary.

In vivid and imaginative detail over the course of ten "books," Milton describes the fall of Adam and Eve from Eden. About a quarter through the epic, he introduces a character named Abdiel, one of the angels who had been tricked by Satan into rebelling against God. Abdiel, whose name translates from Hebrew to "Servant of God," battles alongside the fallen and is cast into hell along with them. There Satan argues that it is "better to rule in Hell than serve in Heaven."

Satan assumes that repentance and reconciliation with God are unavailable to the fallen angels. Abdiel is not convinced and speaks

up against Satan's blasphemous decree: how can one debate justice
with the One who created justice? Abdiel closes his argument by
urging the fallen angels to "hast'n to appease th'incensed Father and
th'incensed Son, while Pardon may be found in time besought."

"But" continues Milton, "[Abdiel's] zeal none seconded." Satan re-
jects the notion that grace is free for all, costing only our pride, only
our self-worship. God's grace topples those things that set themselves
between heaven and earth, like powers and principalities, or authorities and rulers.

Abdiel, "unshaken, unseduc'd, unterrifi'd" among the "innumerable false" and fallen angels, proceeded on his way back toward
heaven. "From amidst them forth he pass'd, long way through
hostile scorn, which he sustain'd superior . . . his back he turned on
those proud tow'rs to swift destruction doomed." He knew that the
way is narrow, and few are those who will find and persist in it
(Matthew 7:14).

Every day during my term of service in the Army, my dog tags reminded me of the encouragement of the apostle Paul in 2 Timothy 4:7-8:

> I have fought the good fight, I have finished the race, I have
> kept the faith. Now there is in store for me the crown of right-
> eousness, which the Lord, the righteous Judge, will award to
> me on that day—and not only to me, but also to all who have
> longed for his appearing.

Those that persevere, the Bible tells us, can expect to find their
reward in heaven. This was Abdiel's experience, who upon passing
"through hostile scorn" and across the great abyss between heaven
and hell is welcomed with joy and acclamations, the heavenly host
rejoicing for "yet one return'd not lost." From the pearly gates, he is led
to the sacred hill where, from the midst of a golden cloud, he hears:

> Servant of God, well done, well hast thou fought the better
> fight, who single hast maintain'd against revolted multitudes
> the Cause of Truth, in Word mightier than they in arms;
>   And for the testimony of Truth hast borne universal re-

proach, far worse to bear than violence: for this was all thy care,
to stand approv'd in sight of God, though Worlds judged thee
perverse.[11]

In Mark Twain's "War Prayer," the congregation judged God's messenger perverse; they thought him to be "a lunatic, because there was
no sense in what he said." Those who (through pride, arrogance, the
euphoric acceptance of a consensus opinion or even through innocent ignorance) reject the message of God where it confronts them
with judgment often perceive those people who *embrace* God's costly
grace as being ideologically perverse, lunatic, even unpatriotic.

Christians who, despite even their own privilege, sense God's call
and respond to it have heard it all throughout history. Jesus pre-
dicted it in his Beatitudes and encouraged his followers to persevere
through it:

> Blessed are you when people insult you, persecute you and
> falsely say all kinds of evil against you because of me. Rejoice
> and be glad, because great is your reward in heaven, for in the
> same way they persecuted the prophets who were before you.
> (Matthew 5:11-12)

Leaving Captain Andrews's office that day, I felt some solidarity
with Abdiel; my spirit was intact, a curious smirk on my face. With
my back toward my old company, dust shook free of my boots as my
feet uttered a silent prayer of joyful gladness . . .

MOVEMENT FIVE

"Peace hath her victories,
No less renowned than war."
JOHN MILTON, SONNET, *TO THE LORD GENERAL CROMWELL*

"We who have witnessed the obscenity of war and experienced
its horror and terrible consequences have an obligation to rise
above our pain and suffering and turn the tragedy of our lives
into a triumph."
RON KOVIC, AUTHOR, *BORN ON THE FOURTH OF JULY*

"God has heard your prayer."
AN ANGEL OF GOD, TO A CENTURION (ACTS 10)

★ ★ ★

Discharge and a
New Charge

✮

BEING EXCOMMUNICATED FROM MY COMPANY was difficult. I'd like to think I was Abdiel, having chosen my path toward reconciling my history with God's boundless love. But in reality, I had been asked to leave, putting pandemonium in my wake as I scratched my head and tried to quench the fire that yet burned in my heart. Captain Andrews and First Sergeant Hartman had reason to be exasperated; the timing was horrible and circumstances were easy to interpret as cowardice. The reality was much less spectacular, and retrospection has made me sympathetic to each of them (less so to Lieutenant Violet). But in the moment, it had all the makings of an epic tragedy.

Driving home that paradigm was how indescribably painful it was to watch my friends deploy without me in August, just a month after being kicked out of my infantry company. Watching my comrades hug their loved ones and choke out teary-eyed goodbyes was heart-wrenching. Finding out later that nearly a dozen of them would not come home to those teary-eyed loved ones was like nothing I had ever experienced. Survivor's guilt infected me without my having stepped on the field of battle with them. I wished my unit actually knew what I wanted: to serve alongside my friends—to not avoid the toils, but to do so without compromising my convictions.

On some level, I was angry at my command. I considered myself a patriot above anything else, save my being a Christian. But my commanders had misinterpreted my patriotism as its opposite—"negative utility" to its mission. I loved my country; I was just not willing to love it more than I did God.

I began to really question whether I could be a patriot. As my military friends became sparse and I increasingly interacted with peace activists, my faith in the "American dream" began to erode.[1] I had done everything I could think of to remain within the confines and the doctrine of the military with my faith intact. I had served my country in good faith. If I could not do so while maintaining my constitutionally protected religious convictions, what value did the American project have?

October 19, 2006, was the day I effectively left the military. I sat in a coffee shop and wrote "Liberty and Justice for All?" about an experience I had in Philadelphia during my summer leave. I reflected on our collective American failure to abide by the inscription on the Liberty Bell, taken from Leviticus 25, to "proclaim freedom for all nations":

> Jeremiah 34:17 holds the grim judgment for those called upon to "proclaim liberty throughout the land to all its inhabitants" [Leviticus 25:10a] and who fail horribly at being the stewards of Liberty for all the inhabitants of the earth:
>
> "Therefore, this is what the LORD says: You have not obeyed me; you have not proclaimed freedom for your fellow countrymen. So now I proclaim 'freedom' for you, declares the LORD— 'freedom' to fall by the sword, plague, and famine. I will make you abhorrent to all the kingdoms of the earth." [NIV 1984][2]

My beliefs were on a long pendulum arch from patriot to pacifist, from self-sacrifice to self-righteousness, from one end of the spectrum to the other. I was ready to sign off on the American project, and all I needed was the pen.

Christian
Peacemakers

✭

THE FIRE IN MY HEART REFUSED TO BE EXTINGUISHED; I still found myself drawn to danger, to the adrenaline of combat and the camaraderie of martial exploits. In the interim between my departure from Captain Andrews' infantry company and my eventual discharge, I applied to participate in a delegation to Palestine with Christian Peacemaker Teams (CPT), a group that offers an organized, nonviolent alternative to war and other forms of lethal inter-group conflict and provides organizational support to persons committed to faith-based nonviolent alternatives in situations where lethal conflict is an immediate reality or is supported by public policy. CPT challenges the church to consider what might happen if peacemakers put as much training and energy into nonviolence as militaries do into violence. They are a kind of alternative army, a mighty league of activists ready to "get in the way of violence."[3] If the Army wouldn't let me serve nonviolently, then they certainly would.

The CPTers didn't know what to make of me; they had never, to my knowledge, had someone so intimately familiar with the military go on one of their delegations. Tensions were particularly high in Palestine at that time, so they made me promise to leave my military ID card at home, for fear it would spark suspicion of my being an Israeli intelligence officer. I was encouraged to grow out my beard, a suggestion I was only too happy to oblige.

We spent much of the early part of our delegation in west Jerusalem, the Israeli side of the city. It felt very Mediterranean, like I could have been anywhere in Europe. The second half of our stay, however, was primarily on the Palestinian side. East Jerusalem reminded me of Tijuana, with poverty levels indicative of a culture in distress. I literally crossed streets from one side to another, like an invisible barrier between two totally different worlds.

Particularly memorable was Hebron, a city in the Palestinian-controlled West Bank dotted by Israeli settlements built in defiance of international law and sentiment. CPT had us visit the Abdullah family, whose home was constantly being pelted by stones from Israeli condominiums on a hill overlooking the house. We talked for over an hour about how the family coped with both the Israeli Defense Forces (IDF) and the settlers. The family never revealed, even subtly, signs of hatred or contempt for the Israeli settlers and soldiers, only a very clear desire to be seen as human.

I was slapped hard in the face by something akin to PTSD as we spoke to the Abdullah family. They reminded me of families I had encountered in Iraq on patrol with an Army platoon not too unlike the IDF units they described. Countless Iraqi faces flashed before my mind's eye, obscene and unforgiving, reflecting the infinite number of others who shared this story of occupation and dehumanization. As the father of the family spoke, his voice, posture, mannerisms and setting changed ceaselessly while I listened attentively and warily to what he had to share. My mind's eye was out of control as I watched the man change from one individual to another. I flew from Iraq to Palestine and back again in fractions of a heartbeat. As I glanced around me at other delegates and CPTers, their dress changed as well. I saw their red caps melt into various Islamic headdresses, then into beige Kevlar helmets and back again. I saw their hands bound in zip-ties; then I saw them cuffing the hands of others around them.

As the Abdullah children served us mint tea, the group sur-rounding me drifted back and forth in my mind from my Army platoon to my CPT delegation. Reality melted into my memory and became reality again until the line between the two blurred into one. Whether Iraq or the West Bank, families were being disrupted and treated with suspicion and hostility. Gender nuances that Westerners didn't fully grasp were being violated; women were being separated from their husbands, daughters from their fathers. Surprise raids came under cover of night.

Of course there were differences between U.S. raids in Iraq and searches conducted by the Israeli Defense Forces, but not as many as one would think. The same rifle I pointed at people in Iraq was being pointed at me in the disputed Palestinian territories.

We left the Abdullah family's house before dark to avoid ha-rassment from the soldiers for violating whatever curfew was in place for the day. We passed an IDF patrol on the way, and I fought off an unexpected and overwhelming urge to shake my head in disgust. I refused to meet the soldiers eye-to-eye or offer my greetings. I wanted to believe that this was because they were falling short in their duties—poor tactical behavior, loose formations, unkempt dress, lack of discipline. I told myself that I expected more of the Israeli Army. I could feel them seeking a brief glance, a "Shalom" or a reas-suring nod, but I rejected their glances, their appeal to my humanity.

It wasn't till much later that I was finally able to give voice what was going on inside me. During an evening roundtable a fellow CPTer, sensing my anxiety, asked me about the IDF patrol. My reply came out so easily, like it had been there the whole time, waiting to escape, so that I might hear it with my ears, since I had blatantly ignored it in my heart: "I see myself in them."

★ ★ ★

For most of my life, on the pendulum between patriotism and pacifism, I had seen the world as a soldier sees it: the world requires justice, accountability, strong and courageous men to fight its wars. When I was converted from a predominantly "patriotic" way of looking at the world to a much more "pacific" way, the pendulum slowly swung until I saw the world in a different light: the world is broken and, more than vengeance and retribution, it needs love and mercy.

I was assigned to rear detachment even as the pendulum was swinging from patriotism to pacifism. I was discharged and said goodbye to the U.S. Army. In Israel, certainty soothed my troubled mind: I was done swinging. I had found my center.

Unbeknownst to me, that was my center, not God's.

As I sat on the roof of CPT's Hebron apartment, processing my vision at the Abdullah family's house, I began to shudder and shake. I did not want to be shown my true nature. I wanted to destroy the Israeli soldiers, to hurt them, to crucify them. How dare they remind me of my brokenness, my pain, my sin? They need to be punished for *their* contempt, *their* ignorance!

Reality broke through the walls I had set up in my mind, the walls that I had painted so beautifully so that I may be protected from the truth. In each of the soldiers I had seen, I had also seen myself.

It broke my heart that I had been spiteful and seen the IDF soldiers as unworthy of my glance. I was now seeing them as they truly deserved to be seen—as created by God, as sharing the same image I bore. More than that, I was acknowledging that I had not forgiven myself for being so uncritical about my role in Iraq, for pride, for apathy, for everything. God had forgiven me the moment I sought his intercession, but I had not forgiven myself.

God was showing me the other side of my rifle's scope. I was the enemy on the other side of my weapon. I was seeing the true damage I had caused just by being a warrior in a worldly battle, a passive participant in an oppression of other human beings.

How could I have known? After all:

I do what I'm taught
and I've been learning a lot
about the violence I'm capable of

. . . 'cause I'm facing enemies
on both sides of the gun[4]

★ ★ ★

To get to an Israeli settlement for a meeting I had scheduled, I had to utilize a bus system that travelled on roads that are restricted to settlers and soldiers. Since I was technically a religious tourist, all I had to do was flash my visa and pay the proper fare.

Palestine has what seems to me to be a very disorganized and disheveled bus system. It was all very informal and unpredictable, nothing like my experience in Honolulu, which has one of the best public transportation systems in the United States—to say nothing of the rigid structure and predictably of military transport. Back in 2001, there had been a massive uprising by Palestinians. The form of transportation I was relying on for my trip to the settlement had been targets for suicide attacks. Sitting on the bus before we took off, I noticed how foggy the windows were. I realized it was for the same reason the windows in our armored Humvees were fogged; they were bulletproof.

I settled into my chair and popped my headphones in as we pulled out of the bay and into the arid Palestinian landscape. My mind wandered to another desert, now painfully aware of the depth of my own frailty and culpability, my childhood innocence having gone AWOL somewhere between my enlistment and watching that first IED explode in front of me:

> When I was young, the smallest trick of light,
> Could catch my eye,
> Then life was new and every new day,
> I thought that I could fly.
> I believed in what I hoped for,

And I hoped for things unseen,
I had wings and dreams could soar,
I just don't feel like flying anymore.
When the stars threw down their spears,
Watered Heaven with their tears[5]

I thought of all the convoys I had been on in Iraq, peering through the same windows blurred by chemicals to protect us. I had seen a lot in the two weeks I was in Palestine—more than I bargained for, and more than I thought I could take. The stars had thrown down explosive spears, and heaven had been watered by the tears of mothers outliving their own children, of sons and daughters killing and being killed in pursuit of worldly peace.

My faith was being stretched, I could not answer why God let all of it happen. I was young and idealistic, and I wanted to believe that change was imminent. The pace at which the world changes is frustrating.

For some reason, I was struck with another bus experience I had just eight months prior. The lyrics and artist were different this time around, but the song God was singing to me was exactly the same.

The struggles go on
The wisdom I lack
The burdens keep piling
Up on my back
So hard to breathe
To take the next step
The mountain is high
I wade in the depths
Yearning for grace
And hoping for peace
Dear God increase!

My impatient feelings of hoping for peace and yearning for grace were being burdened by my own expectations. But my hope needed to be in God, not in what fruit I could hope to see from my labor.

I was beginning to learn that my frustration was in not being able to see change before my own eyes. I had assumed God worked on my own schedule. I didn't know any better than to expect to see the fruits of the labor for peace and justice. The world groaned, and I wanted to believe that God would hear and respond in my own time.

It is a long, hard lesson to stop expecting change. Work gains us nothing in the face of God, and yet faith does call us to action. We are known by how we love others, and that is only made visible by what we do and say. But the catch is to act in faith without expectation of reward—even the reward of seeing the change we hope for. I have been to too many angry protests to cling to the expectation that the good that God is doing in our world will be worked out in my own lifetime; evil is simply too pervasive. Anything I do, I try to do with patient love, not breathless anticipation.

The 2006 CPT delegation lasted through the first week of Advent, the season in which we wait for the Christ child to arrive. Sometimes, though our heart screams, our feet must remain patiently prayerful. The tiniest mustard seed can produce "the largest of all garden plants" (Mark 4:32); the smallest act of patient love can produce great fruit. The radish is closely related to the mustard; even the most "radical" activist waits expectantly, as we do during Advent. Humble baby steps mark the path to justice. After all, it is a child who leads us.

New Missions

✯

ON MARCH 16, 2007, I SPOKE AT THE Christian Peace Witness for Iraq at the National Cathedral in Washington, D.C.[6] I had nearly convinced myself that I had escaped my demons. I was sure I had come to forgive myself for all the things I had done and failed to do in my martial struggle against flesh and blood (Ephesians 6:12). My troubled past now seemed inconsequential. The images and memories from that period had mostly ceased in their assault against my waking mind.

Exposing myself deliberately to the emotions surrounding my service was an active embrace of vulnerability. After my discharge, I had moved from Honolulu to Camden, New Jersey, which at the time was the most violent city in America. I feared most a life of complacency, a life that denied my past and ignored my transgressions, a life that refused to acknowledge the presence and urgency of evil. Occasionally, I would wonder if

> Maybe redemption has stories to tell
> Maybe forgiveness is right where you fell
> Where can you run to escape from yourself?[7]

As realistic as I thought I was being, I couldn't have imagined how difficult it would be to actually confront the violence of my past.

I was to read the words of a fellow soldier and recognized conscientious objector, Joshua Casteel, who had been an interrogator at Abu Ghraib just months after a prisoner abuse scandal there broke.[8] The weight and significance of the event wasn't apparent to me until it came time to rehearse what I would have to read on stage in front of nearly three thousand fellow followers of Jesus. I hadn't been given the text of Joshua's testimony until the day of the event, and I couldn't stomach what I would be expected to read.

An interrogator has a different experience from mine as a forward observer. There are much fewer degrees of separation between myself and the violence I committed on behalf of the American people and way of life. Casteel described experiencing great moral upheaval when he pointed his weapon at three young shepherd boys. He was in Iraq just a few months when he recognized the obscenity of war; it had taken me a trip across the world to Hebron to understand how dirty my hands were, how morally compromised my conscience reminded me that I was. How could I read this?

Casteel's words were simple and struck me at my core. I wished to be as sensitive to those boys' humanity after just one experience.

I wandered the church. I had to find something to keep me busy, to keep the figure at bay who was pounding at the door to my heart. Eventually, I found an out-of-the way chapel with nobody inside. I plugged in my MP3 player and put on some music from The Psalters,[9] hoping to soothe my mind—or at least to keep it distracted.

I passed a fresco in a side hallway and let my eyes meander over it as my ears filled with music. Christ was newly emerged from his grave as two Roman guards reclined against a nearby set of steps. My eyes rested on the soldiers; they seemed so unimpressed by Jesus' emergence from the tomb. The same smoldering contempt I had felt toward the Israeli soldiers began to bubble up within me, quickly accompanied by a battle of words raging within me about soldiering and Christianity.

My eyes wandered back to Christ; the breath left my lungs as my heart broke, rent in two by the image before me. Clear voices ran through my head:

"Even these, who flogged him?"

"Yes."

I nearly stumbled to the floor with grief and pain. Images of Iraq flooded my mind again: a platoon sergeant with his hand locked around a man's throat; a squad leader on a rooftop, shooting a woman with no weapon in her hand; an infantryman punching a man in the stomach while his hands were cuffed behind his back; the man's expression as he doubled over; a set of cross hairs settling on a mud hut outside Kirkuk, fodder for the howitzers behind me.

"Even these, who struck his face and cast lots for his clothes?"

"Yes."

I shuffled to a chair further into the chapel. Tears threatened to swell and redden my face as I slumped in the chair, pulling my hood low. The chair sat before a candelabra, an altar of sorts. "Come all you weary,"[10] the Psalters sang to me.

"Even these, who pierced his very heart?"

"Yes. They know not what they do."

Jesus was speaking to the Accuser in my place; it was one of the last things he said on the cross, about the very soldiers who crucified him (Luke 23:34). Even as I felt bombarded by desire to hate those who hated him, I was reminded that I too had once been an enemy of God, piercing his very heart (John 19:34). I remembered that he came to me even then, that I too needed that unquenchable enemy-love Jesus taught us. I remembered that it was also a soldier who displayed greater faith than anyone in Israel, and a soldier who looked upon the crucified Jesus and said, "Surely this was a righteous man" (Luke 23:47; cf. Matthew 27:54; Mark 15:39).

So many have returned from Iraq and Afghanistan deeply conflicted about what they have done. For many years, the suicide, substance abuse and homelessness rates of veterans have skyrocketed. Torn between allegiances and oaths and empty promises, this generation of combat veterans groans.

On both sides of the just war–pacifism argument are stuck virtuous and unassuming individuals trying to figure it out. They are tired of being preached at or accused of generalizations and made victims of stereotypes. Few service members truly grasp the demands being placed on them when they sign a Department of Defense contract. During my CO claim, I had been misunderstood not just by pious and patriotic Americans insisting that God is a warrior, but also by members of peace churches who insist that Christians have no place in the military. I had internalized anxieties and frustrations about military service as a front to partition myself off from my own guilt. A generation groans against the pressures of patriotism and pacifism, as though the two are mutually exclusive.

Eventually, quaking from grief and repentance, I approached the altar slowly. The parable of the Pharisee and the tax collector came to mind again:

> To some who were confident of their own righteousness and looked down on everyone else, Jesus told this parable: "Two men went up to the temple to pray, one a Pharisee and the other a tax collector. The Pharisee stood by himself and prayed: 'God, I thank you that I am not like other people—robbers, evildoers, adulterers—or even like this tax collector. I fast twice a week and give a tenth of all I get.'
>
> "But the tax collector stood at a distance. He would not even look up to heaven, but beat his breast and said, 'God, have mercy on me, a sinner.'
>
> "I tell you that this man, rather than the other, went home justified before God. For all those who exalt themselves will be humbled, and those who humble themselves will be exalted."
> (Luke 18:9-14)

That night, however, I heard a different lesson. I knew that I had to approach the altar of lights and pray on my knees. Wiping the snot from my beard, choking out sobs and coming to my feet, I took three steps and fell before the stand of lights. Remembering my time in Hebron and what God had shown me there, I begged again for forgiveness but also for the strength to be what I had asked to be on the night of my baptism: a living sacrifice. It would be painful, it would be angering . . . it would be redemption.

★ ★ ★

Surprisingly, I read Joshua's words without falter. When my segment of the liturgy was complete, I proceeded to my seat, off to the right of the altar, out of the view of most of those gathered there. The segment that followed me included a reflection on a soldier who had taken his life after returning from war. Jeffrey Lucy had told his sister that he felt like he was becoming a monster. His parents, Joyce and Kevin Lucy, found him hanging by a garden hose in their basement. He had wrapped the rubber twice around his neck, to make double sure he'd put this world and its monstrosities behind him.[11]

I broke down like never before. My face was painted in briny tears, my face convulsing in grief as though I was having a concentrated seizure. I haven't wept so violently before or since. I hid from view as best I could, since, you know, real soldiers don't cry.

I found later that Joshua's words came across as almost confessional, maybe from one soldier on behalf of many. I never would propose to speak for others, but if the amount of emails I get from other war-weary warriors is any indication, there is a flood of grief waiting to be released, held stubbornly in place by society's collective emotional impotency. A large number of us are groaning under the pressure to suck it up and drive on, all while we are falling apart and crashing down.

★ ★ ★

The road to redemption is never easy. My experience of it has been less like the road to Emmaus, where two disciples enjoyed Jesus' company unawares, and more like the road to Jericho, where a good Samaritan came upon a man who had been beaten and left for dead.

I constantly felt beat up, either by my own self-doubt or by others who unconsciously villainized or venerated me for my service. My impression has been that service members are vilified by the "left" for their complicity in organized violence, and are venerated by the "right" for their willingness to serve. I am convinced that both reactions have nearly equal destructive capacity.

When service members are called heroes, they are called to a standard of living that is impossible to achieve, especially given what they experience in combat. The other end of the spectrum, however, is to call service members monsters. This is equally inaccurate but much easier for soldiers to believe about themselves in dark moments. As a soldier I could never be just human, just a man trying to live a life of faith; I was always either hero or monster to just about everyone I met. The greatest challenge in my life has been simply to find a community of fellow believers who know me not as Logan, "Combat Veteran," but as Logan, "Friend."

I was very lucky, during my CO application process, to have been introduced to people from Camden, New Jersey, who were living in intentional community with one another. During PAPA Fest Chris Haw invited me to live with them for a little while, to decompress and rebuild my life. In 2008, Camden had the highest crime rate in the United States, with 2,333 violent crimes per 100,000 people, while the national average was 455 per 100,000. I had grown up in the Southern California suburbs, so Camden, with its high poverty and violent crime rates, would be a pretty significant shift.

There is nowhere that I can imagine that would have been as powerfully transforming as living in America's most violent city. During my time in Camden I was confronting the history of violence in my life. I knew that I could have found an easier, less challenging place to live and study, but God put me in Camden. Maybe it was a test of my pacifism.

The first time I had that thought, I was bicycling through town after dark during what must have been spring break for the local schools. A young kid pulled up alongside me and nodded in a way that made me believe he was trying to intimidate me. He couldn't have been older than sixteen, and no more than 150 pounds. He kept looking over his shoulder, which led me to believe there was a pack of other kids he was trying to prove himself to.

My earphones were in, so I played like I didn't hear him. Incensed, he raised his voice and flashed what looked to be a metal pipe. My heartbeat shot up, and I went into a kind of emergency mode. I knew he couldn't hit me with his far hand, so I assessed that I could bump him off his bike and just pedal off, avoiding a more serious confrontation. But what would I do if I did knock him off his bike? Would biking off be the loving thing to do to my newfound enemy? Could I even ram him in the first place?

Again, I'm a pacifist; I'm not stupid. I wasn't going to invite disaster by simply doing nothing. Instead, I looked him straight in the eye, acknowledging him and what he seemed to want to do, but not bending to fear. I kept pedaling at the same speed, hoping he wouldn't take a swing. And he didn't, thanks be to God.

I was reminded of the pool of blood at my feet in Mosul, that the violence in others isn't always easy to distinguish from our own. Maybe it was good that I had avoided getting hit by a pipe with my dignity intact, but I was not innocent. Living in Camden, I was constantly reminding myself of that fact. In a way, the year I spent there was a kind of incubation for me while God continued to call me to my vocation, which I was learning, since turning to Anthony so many months prior, was wrapped up in faith and service.

Fighting off my acute tendencies to do violence gave me a purpose for some time, enough to reconstitute the person that I was before I had deployed. When others come home from war, particularly in a poor economy, the deep sense of purpose and belonging that the military provided is lost, leaving many veterans wandering, metaphorically, like Cain—painfully aware of their past, crying out that their burden is too great. The focus required of me in Camden kept my mind where it belonged, in communion with others, with a church and with the One who marked me not for condemnation but protection.[12]

Centurion's Guild

★

SOMETIME IN 2007, I WAS INVITED to facilitate a discussion at The Simple Way in Philadelphia, across the Delaware River from Camden,[13] following a screening of the *The Ground Truth*. At the end of the showing, I was asked by someone from the pacifist-inclined audience, "What can people do to support service members?"

I had heard enough of the sloganeering around "supporting the troops." Most vets appreciate the basic sentiment, but in my experience talking with other veterans, there is a pretty strong consensus that the yellow-ribbon pins and magnets that people wear to "support the troops" fall far short of the gravity of military service. Supporting troops takes more time, resources and energy than a cheap ribbon can possibly represent. With this in mind, maybe I was a little jaded, but I didn't want to just dismiss the question—not the least of which because it was honest: if the yellow ribbon magnet isn't enough, then what should folks be doing?

I still don't really have an answer, although I hope this book is part of it. How am I, one veteran whose experience in combat can probably be described as mild, supposed to answer such a deep question? How could civilians support people with such incredibly significant, and often traumatic, experiences in ways that are healthy and theologically credible?

The question sat with me for a while.

During my own processing, I met a number of other COs—most (if not all) of whom were also Christians. Some were more politically charged than others, but they by and large did a great job of listening to me and guiding me along the way, both in the administrative stuff but also the theological questioning I was going through. They directed me to resources that would both challenge and encourage me. They walked alongside me without judgment or condemnation, even though, unlike me, most of them had sought discharge.[14] What if that experience could be duplicated for others? What if nobody had to walk the road alone?[15]

An idea eventually crystallized in my mind to conceive a kind of guild for fellow centurions wrestling between faith and service as I and others had. Centurion's Guild finally entered the world in January 2008 with four founding members and a mission to "protect and defend prospective, current, and former service members while bearing true faith and allegiance to God."[16]

From the outset, our mission was not too different than it had been when we all wore the uniform of United States military personnel. In fact, one of us was still in service. We all felt strongly that there was room for improvement in the way the church dealt with members who bore the yoke of national service. Tired of false dichotomies and uncritical assumptions about war and peace, we focused on responding pastorally to others like us who were trying, just like the military chaplaincy, to "serve God and country" (in that order).

But Centurion's Guild is not the answer; it is just a beginning. We all, civilian and service connected alike, have a duty to think more deeply and converse more meaningfully about Christian faith and military service, about how our identities as both citizens and Christians sometimes conflict with, but at other times complement, one another. We need to peel the two apart long enough to discern where church ends and state begins, and when our duty to God trumps our obedience to country. I promise you, it is not as simple as you might think.

***

I am learning that not only is redemption an unpaved road; it often leads you in circles. I wished (on some level) to rid myself of my past. The last thing I wanted to do was to be reminded of my own transgressions, of failing to think and act critically about my role as an artilleryman in the most powerful and destructive armed force the world has, up until this point, ever known. But the Spirit had other plans.

During the Cornerstone Music Festival in Bushnell, Illinois, in 2009, I was a volunteer at the CPT table. Cornerstone is often held around the Fourth of July weekend. The evening of July 3 I went to bed relatively early after a long day. My tent was near a dirt road, close to one of the stages. I hadn't thought through the placement very well, certainly not in light of a recent diagnosis of PTSD.

All night, people buzzed by my tent in golf carts and set off firecrackers along the road. Each pop and bang sent shockwaves of dark memories through my body. The golf carts added to the sensory melee I was experiencing. I was hyped up on adrenaline and posttraumatic stress. I paid little mind to the fact that it was my three year re-birthday, that I could have remembered my entrance into the body of Christ instead of been re-traumatized. God could have given the fireworks a deeper, more profound "bang" . . .

I don't know how or why I lasted as long as I did, but by 3 a.m., I emerged from my tent without a wink of sleep, body and limbs quaking in episodic fervor. My heart raced, and I paced around hoping to God that the images that had clawed their way into my head would be released. I felt like the possessed man from Mark 5, pacing around a graveyard, surrounded by death, crying out and afflicted by overwhelming pain.[17]

I left a note with the other CPTers I had volunteered with that I could not stay, packed up my stuff and drove off toward home. My first stop would be the Veterans Hospital for an impromptu visit to a counselor.

On the road, my phone buzzed with a new email from Shane, about a trip to Rutba, Iraq, he was planning with others who had been there with him in 2003. Greg Barrett, an author hoping to capture a reunion story, was organizing the trip.[18]

For the rest of the drive, I couldn't get Iraq out of my head. Was Shane inviting me? If he was, wouldn't I be crazy to go back? Wouldn't I just be inviting danger as an Iraq veteran returning to his combat theater *while we were still at war*?

At the end of my drive, I replied to Shane asking him to keep me abreast of the conversations. He forwarded my email to the team planning the trip. The next thing I knew I was on the manifest.

In January 2010, I found myself back in Hawaii, getting ready to return to Iraq. Church of the Crossroads in Hawaii, which has a rich history of supporting service members in the midst of war (one year they had provided sanctuary to over thirty service members whose conscience prohibited them from serving in Vietnam),[19] had offered its blessing and support to my trip, but I still had significant hesitations. My role there was undefined; I had no idea what I would be doing.

It's difficult describing what drew me to the trip. Something (or Someone) called to me, a whisper carried by the desert winds. Maybe I would find the man I lost in combat. Maybe redemption still had a story to tell. The closest I could come to putting it to words came in the form of a song:

> I'm holding on to the hope that one day this could be made right.
> I've been shipwrecked, and left for dead, and I have seen the darkest sights. . . .
> But oh my heart still burns, tells me to return, and search the fading light.[20]

Something in me wanted to *do* something. I needed a mission, some direction, anything to give me a sense of purpose. But all I could do was appreciate the opportunity to be present once again to the wilderness, both within and without. It was a needed exercise in patience and humility.

Gospel of Rutba

⭑

OUR TEAM WAS MADE UP of CPTers Cliff Kindy, Peggy Gish, Weldon Nisly, our Iraqi guide Sami Rasouli, videographer Jamie Moffett,[21] Greg, Shane and me. We met up in Jordan and immediately went about trying to secure visas to cross the border into Iraq. It eventually became clear that it would be unwise to reveal my history in the U.S. military, for my own safety and that of the team but also for our hosts in Iraq. Even if the folks we stayed with were sympathetic to a soldier returning to their theater of combat to explore what reconciliation looks like, we could still get kidnapped—or, worse, our hosts could be harmed. I would have to keep my cards very close to my chest.

It was a headache waiting for word from the Iraqi embassy in Jordan about whether we would get access. The route was a kind of backdoor, since the U.S. Consulate in Washington, D.C., had failed to pull through in a timely manner, though U.S. forces still effectively controlled the borders. Sure enough, when things finally worked out and we got to No Man's Land between Iraq and Jordan, a small U.S. Army convoy met us and insisted we needed armed escorts. It didn't occur to them that, given the circumstances, the attention they drew to us would be more harmful than helpful.

Returning to Iraq in the midst of war was surreal. I think I spent most of my time in a kind of trance, trying my best to watch my words. It was very hard not to "smoke and joke" with some of the Iraqi forces, who had been trained by a friend's Navy unit that had left Rutba a few months before we arrived.

We were hosted for the duration of our stay by a group of staff doctors near the hospital in Rutba where Shane, Cliff and Weldon were treated in 2003, the hospital that had been damaged by American bombs.[22] I introduced myself in Arabic as a student who was studying peace, an act that garnered a lot of grins and nods.

There were occasional gunshots and distant explosions, but the scariest moment for me came when one of the police officers acting as our guard detail asked Cliff if he had ever killed anyone. My heart leapt into my throat: What if he asked me the same question? Would I lie? Could I? I tried to pretend not to notice, but I heard Cliff laugh and respond gently that he had not.

Cliff and the others knew that I had been conflicted about accompanying them, of the mystery surrounding the how and why I was there. They also knew the difficulty I faced in remaining silent about myself; it was as if I was only partially there, as if I was not fully present in the moments we shared with Iraqis we met. Cliff graciously redirected the conversation to make sure it did not drift in my direction.

The last day before we were set to head back to Jordan, we visited a boys' school not far from the hospital. We arrived and had a chat with the principal and faculty. I'll never forget something the principal said, in reference to the unity between Islam and Christianity: "Our Creator tells us that education is equivalent to worship." I wondered if something like it was behind my own parents' constant encouragement to take my education seriously or, more importantly, my own view of the sacramentality of education. Worship is so much more than the songs we sing or the words we pray. God can be glorified by our actions as well as by our faith. Educating children, standing in solidarity with the disadvantaged, persevering with the oppressed—all are acts of worship toward Emmanuel, the God-with-us.

I fought back tears thinking how right the principal was.

Outside, after our more formal greeting with the faculty, the boys formed up and loudly chanted the Iraqi national anthem for us. We shook their hands and said hello, and I asked a few how old they were and what their names were. They were pretty excited that I knew some Arabic, and I was too. That changed, however, when it came time to share some of the gifts we brought for the kids.

The boys all huddled around a red-headed boy, about six years old. Apparently, he would get the first pick of all the items in our bag. After him, his older brother would get to rummage through it, before the rest of the gifts were distributed as fairly as possible among the rest of the school. The redhead was really timid. He seemed to take some convincing to go ahead and take his pick of the loot. I asked our interpreter how they chose this particular student to have first dibs. He told me that the child and his brother were orphans; their father had been killed by American forces.

✳ ✳ ✳

God forced a thorn into my side all the way to the hilt. The man I watched die in Iraq that cold night so long ago was an orphan. His two young daughters were orphaned by war too. My heart was being forced through a rusty paper shredder. My breaking heart made a noise that cried out to God, and God cried out right back at me.

I couldn't find any words; I just stared blankly at the boy. My mind at that moment was desolate, devoid of anything resembling a coherent thought. It was like Holy Saturday, the day sandwiched between Good Friday and Easter Sunday, when the whole of creation waited silently and anxiously for the resurrection. I wondered, with the church that day, if all was lost, if the world had hope left to speak of.

I knew I couldn't let anyone see me if I broke down, so I bottled up my emotions. If I moved, it was because I was directed to. I was lost awkwardly between the waking world of light and the foreboding darkness of night. The feeling persisted mercilessly through the rest of the day, as we heard from local families and sheikhs about horrible things that American service members had done—defecating on Qurans, detaining minors and women, shooting at people indiscriminately. My soul was decimated; my tongue clung to the roof of my mouth. I could neither rebut nor be reconciled. All I could do was listen. It was January; Advent had come and gone; why must reconciliation wait any longer? Listening to these horrible stories featuring centurions like me, I felt like Pharaoh all over again, only this time my heart was not hardened but broken.

"*Even these?*" I heard once again.

"*Yes,*" Came the reply.

The next day, as we sped off toward Amman and the various worlds we had all left behind, it began to pour rain. The deluge continued until I had put the desert wilderness far behind me. I had gone from the garden to the desert and back again. Again.

✶ ✶ ✶

I couldn't be sure if what drew me to this second "deployment" to Iraq was a choir of coaxing angels or a murder of crowing Sirens, like those that beckoned to Odysseus, a veteran of the Trojan War who spent ten arduous years fighting to get home to his loved ones.[23] As his ship neared the Sirens, they sang to him about his conflicted martial past. He ordered his men to stuff their ears with beeswax and tie him to the mast of their ship so that they could sail safely past. Today's veterans face Siren calls of our own: depression, substance abuse and suicide. They threaten to break us on the rocks of our own moral misgivings about what we've done and what we've failed to do. The temptation among veterans to self-contempt or willful ignorance is its own Siren call. If not confronted, PTSD and moral injury can destroy lives and erode relationships. Josh Garrels's song "Ulysses" poignantly illustrates the precariousness of the odyssey home from the battlefield:

Trouble has beset my ways, and wicked winds have blown. Sirens call my name, say they'll ease my pain, and break me on the stone.

Like Odysseus and his crew, the church congregates week after week in capsized ships[24] to navigate the homeward journey of faith in this upside-down world. Like the ark that Noah built to navigate the Great Flood, we sail wanderously, not sure exactly to where or for how long.

I'm sailing home to You, I won't be long . . .
So tie me to the mast of this old ship and point me home[25]

* * *

Two months after our team navigated back from the water-logged wilderness of Rutba, I testified at the Truth Commission on Conscience in War at the Riverside Church in New York City.[26] I shared about my two deployments to Iraq (first as a soldier and again as a peacemaker) and reflected on how my trip to Rutba, though painful, helped me feel one heartbeat closer to redemption. My heart still beats, urging me to return, again and again, to redemption. Sometimes the circuitous journey of faith brings us, overwhelmed by bruises and brokenness, closer to Jericho. Other times we draw near Emmaus, our hearts yearning and burning to do the work our heavenly Commander entrusts to us. For Christian soldiers, caught up in the war in our hearts and minds, the trials are legion and the Sirens close at hand. But at the center of the church is our mast, which is Christ. Veterans need their fellow voyagers to tie them to the mast in order to withstand the temptation of ignoring their pasts, of letting time haphazardly heal the hidden wounds of war. We need compassion, a suffering with.

The rains that came on our drive out of Rutba made me wonder how long I'd float aimlessly as I wrestled with my own military history. Forty days, like Noah? Ten years, like Odysseus? The first time it drizzled after the Flood, Noah must have panicked; the rain had swallowed up so much life beneath the hull of his hastily constructed ark. Was the deluge upon him once again? But God has a curious way of guiding us. He takes us through the desert in order to arrive at the garden; there is no rainbow without rain, no healing without suffering, no reconciliation from sin without a reminder thereto. We arrive at God's promise having persevered *despite* the pain; the path to Emmaus takes us through Jericho.[27]

The church is God's reminder that, despite the storm, all is not lost. Nobody is alone in the painful but promising journey of faith. May we together, singing as one, drown out the Sirens' serenade with our own song:

O come, O come, Emmanuel . . .

Epilogue

★

I STILL WRESTLE WITH WHAT TO DO when my nation does things that I cannot in good conscience support, things that make me not just cringe but quake with disgust. Our country killed more civilians than insurgents. Our country dropped bombs on the children's ward in Rutba. We are all responsible. The "some" that Heschel speaks of, who witnessed it most directly, the ones pulling the triggers and flicking the switches, are falling on their swords at greater rates than those who are falling by the sword; in 2009 and 2010 alike, the raw number of suicides among active duty service members outnumbers the amount of combat fatalities in Iraq and Afghanistan combined.[1] Upon discharge, the proportions skyrocket: over seventeen veterans end their own lives every day.[2]

> forgotten men on long forgotten roads
> so far to go, so few to share the load
> everyone has come and gone
> but the road is still a thousand miles long
> and the worst, at most, is my very best[3]

Time does not heal all the hidden wounds of war, and the victims of our bombs are not the only ones who suffer. To this day, the sights and smells of war haunt me in my dreams. My compatriots and I have the highest rate of suicide of any demographic in our nation's history. Post-traumatic stress is our penance, traumatic brain injury our torment. We cry out with Cain, our fratricidal forebear, "Our punishment is too great to bear!"

Our likeness with God having been tarnished by repeated deployments and the deafening silence that too often greets us upon our return, we veterans cry out.[4] We who are all that we can be, we few and proud, we who flogged him, pierced his side and mistreated him as a detainee, we find ourselves the objects of Jesus' prayer on the cross: "Father forgive them, for they know not what they do."

Too many of us remain in exile even upon our return from war. We wander restlessly through a moral wasteland, our character fragmented and fragile. Some of us remain trapped by our martial experience, exiled to live vicariously through our last deployment, the last fix of adrenaline and camaraderie seldom matched outside combat.

If we darken the halls of a church, we sit in the back, beating our chest with the tax collector in Luke's Gospel, "God have mercy on us, sinners!" We know too well the first part of the prayer of the centurion of Matthew 8:9: "Lord, I am not worthy to receive you." But we require the rest of the church to remind us of its conclusion: "Only say the word and I shall be healed."[5]

To assume that the challenges facing veterans is as easy as throwing more money at the Veterans Administration is not doing anybody any good. The issue begins in our hearts. It begins with how we talk about faith and service. We in the church must be prepared to help our congregants discern credibly between the virtue of charity and the compulsion to service. To what extent has the military appropriated the language of sacrifice, loyalty and obedience? To what extent have we abdicated it?

My favorite class in high school was an introduction to psychology, led by a white-haired thread of a man whom I admired. He taught us that love and hate are actually not opposites but emotionally related.

Hate, he would tell us, is really just frustrated love. The opposite of love is indifference. Think about it: when a child says in anger that she hates her mom or dad, does she really mean it? Fates remain intertwined when we hate; we are still involved, which means we can (and often want to) be reconciled. The angel Abdiel was right!

My teacher was a very energetic and boisterous man, but when he talked about indifference, his entire demeanor would change. He would say solemnly, "Don't ever stop caring. When that happens, your soul begins to die." Martin Luther King Jr. spoke viscerally of his country out of love. The great disappointment he felt was in fact not possible without great love. We must not love our country shallowly, as a great number of pundits do, speaking casually about it as a gift from God to the world. This is a misunderstanding of how God has ordained nations. Nations are accidental to creation, not an organic part of God's plan for the world but a contingent reality in place because of the fallenness of our world. Like pastors, ordained things serve a finite purpose. In the hereafter, we will finally be that nation of priests our spiritual forbears were called toward. We will no longer need nationality or worldly citizenship.

Romans 13 uses the language of ordination in relation to the nations because it is something that God has commissioned to keep our corruption in check, something that has no place in the final reality and ultimate end that we are moving toward. That Paul writes to the Romans from prison acknowledges the finitude of these ordained structures to actually serve justice and honor God. Insofar as the nation claims to be immune to the trappings of time and the limitations of this-worldly love, it is an idol. Inasmuch as a person claims to love their country but cannot turn their eyes to its faults, they are idolaters. Nonetheless, there is still space for love. Satan was wrong!

Patriotism, a moderated love for our land and its features, is good, but nationalism, the love of homeland to the exclusion of others, is not. The late Pope John Paul II made this distinction:

Nationalism involves recognizing and pursuing the good of

one's own nation alone, without regard for the rights of others, patriotism, on the other hand, is a love for one's native land that accords rights to all other nations equal to those claimed for one's own. Patriotism, in other words, leads to a properly ordered social love.[6]

I know people who have left their country in a kind of protest, but they are still seen in their adopted country as "expatriates." We can never fully undo our own cultural formation, however troubling it might be for us. We are stuck with our national identity until the end of this world, when Jesus returns to replace it with something that will consume all these accidental and superficial identities we embody.

So how do we love our land without becoming either cynics or idolaters? Love is not boastful or proud; it does not dishonor others (1 Corinthians 13:4-5). To love our country is not to sing its praises blindly but to recognize its strengths as well as its weaknesses. True love is critical without being contemptuous. Love refuses to look past mistakes, to ignore injustice. God does not love us shallowly, nor should we have love for others that is trivial. No, we should love our country as much as we are able by setting healthy limitations on our expressions thereof. We need to recognize that love for country is not limitless, that Caesar only gets what's his after we've given to God what belongs to God. Once we've rendered to God, there may be only scraps left for Caesar, which we should give with love and respect (Matthew 22:21).

Conscience needs to be a central part of our discernment as Christians. Sometimes we put too much hope in the state or its agents to be the change the church itself needs to be. I don't like the saying, "Be the change you want to see," though I have much respect for Gandhi for saying it. I think it can be misleading, since it can allow us to assume that change happens by our own effort. That is rarely the case. Most major social changes have been the collective initiative of entire movements.

A friend of mine is always reminding me that "people are always just waiting on marching orders," which is a way of saying they just want to be told what to do:

I don't wanna know if the answers aren't easy
so just bring [the law] down from the mountain to me[7]

I know all about marching orders, but it's not what people need. There are no easy answers; what works for one community doesn't necessarily work for another. What is needed is new energy, a way for churches to join in the movement of the Spirit. The imagery of a pendulum has helped me remember that I will probably never settle on precisely what I think about church and state, and that's OK; the longer the pendulum swings, the closer I come to center, the more I inhabit the middle ground between patriot and pacifist. Besides, life is motion; when I stop moving it probably means this body has expired . . .

Instead of "being the change," the church must participate in the change *God* is making in the world. We need to be aware of how ambition can come close to idolatry, how our actions aren't necessarily what's important, but how (and whether) they point to God.

We need to remember that the center of attention is supposed to be Jesus, not us. It's not merely about what we are doing, but what God is doing *through and with us.* Thinking otherwise not only ignores the presence and power of God, but also allows us to assume that our hands and feet *are* God, and not simply means used *by* God.

We shouldn't be afraid to remind ourselves of our scars, our frailties. Doing so might help to curb ambition. Why do you think Paul suggested we boast in our weaknesses? It is a fine balance, however, between self-loathing and arrogance, and it takes a keen eye to chart a safe course. I know it has been hard for me. Not only do I struggle with internal doubts, but there are always people, as Pastor John reminded me, "that will agree or disagree with you," people who are ready to tear you down or build you up. If you are being held up by your own power, you'll fall. As a professor constantly reminds me, "It's about God, stupid."

We are afraid of what we will see when the veil of blissful ignorance is removed from our eyes, when we glimpse the depth of our
sinfulness. "But whenever anyone turns to the Lord, the veil is taken
away" (2 Corinthians 3:16). When it is, Jesus hands us a mirror in the
Word of God, against which none are without fault. The distressing
sin-scarred image in the mirror is us. Not them, us. The men and
women who, in fear, throw accusations and hatred, bullets and
bombs, who insist upon punitive justice instead of restorative justice,[8]
do not realize that they are directing outward the rage they feel
toward themselves, the innermost depths of their own despair.

Sometimes the ugliness that stares back at us from the mirror of
God's Word is overwhelming. If we deny soldiers the opportunity to
grieve what they see when they scrutinize themselves, by blud-
geoning them with our own platitudinous gratitude and "sanctimonious trivialities,"[9] we are complicit when they collapse under the
pressure of self-contempt and moral fragmentation.

I am guilty of sin, just as my enemy is. We are each made in the
image of God, friend and foe alike. When I am able to admit I am
broken and in need of grace, Jesus helps me to see others as I see
myself—even as he removes the scars and sin and brings us together
beautifully restored. That is our commission: to remind others of our
common humanity, our shared brokenness and the inherent value in
our likeness with God. Once we are able to accept that commission,
we realize that Jesus is still holding up a mirror to us, only now we
see him looking back at us. His temple is us. We see with his eyes. We
see and embrace him within us and within others. The stones fall
from our hands, we are reborn:

> We all, who with unveiled faces contemplate the Lord's glory,
> are being transformed into his image with ever-increasing glory.
> (2 Corinthians 3:18)

Appendix A

Justice, War and Conscience

☆

JUST WAR IS A BODY OF BELIEFS, often religiously based, that outlines a number of criteria defining what constitutes a war that is just. Because it developed over time, it is difficult to say officially what those criteria are; different schools of thought, faith communities and Christian denominations differ on which criteria make up the core principles of just war. Several, however, are pretty well established as central to the just war tradition:

- *Just Cause/Right Intent:* Purpose must be to restore justice or preserve the peace. Vengeance, profiteering and other forms of national self-interest are forbidden by just war principles.

- *Likelihood of Success:* A just war cannot be a lost cause; it must have a reasonable expectation that the good being fought for will prevail.

- *Last Resort:* All other viable means of diplomacy and negotiation must be exhausted before a just war commences.

- *Declaration of War by a Legitimate Authority:* Clear statement must outline conditions for surrender.

- *Protection of Noncombatants:* Noncombatants must be immune from indiscriminate violence.

- *Proportionality:* The violence that a just war produces must not be greater than the violence it seeks to constrain.

Just war has its origins in Cicero, a Roman political figure who influenced Augustine of Hippo, whom the church often credits (rather misleadingly) for having conceived the tradition. In reality, Augustine made scattered remarks throughout his many works about the possibility of a war being just in Christian terms, but his comments were by and large pastoral replies to government officials and high-ranking soldiers. Just war originally conceived in the church was not a means of reconciling war with Christian belief but with the moral and spiritual fragmentation that soldiers suffer in war.

The just war "doctrine" never existed as a systematic framework before probably the twelfth century. It was then that Thomas Aquinas, a Dominican monk, methodically outlined when violence might be considered justified. It was not until a seventeenth-century Dutch theologian named Hugo Grotius wrote *On the Law of War and Peace* that just war began to be incorporated into national and global political considerations.

At the same time Grotius was writing, the American colonies were becoming increasingly discontent with English rule. Colonies like Pennsylvania were heavily populated by Anabaptist groups like the Quakers and the Amish, who had been severely persecuted in Europe before fleeing to the colonies for religious freedom. Their influence was significant enough that James Madison wrote into the first draft of the Second Amendment to the U.S. Constitution a protection for people "religiously scrupulous" to be guaranteed the right to refuse to bear arms. It passed in the House, but the Senate watered it down on August 14, 1789, for fear that a too-powerful federal government could dictate those who were "religiously scrupulous," involuntarily prohibit them from bearing arms, and thereby dissolve state militias (which existed "to prevent the establishment of a *standing army,* the bane of liberty"—emphasis mine).

Contemporary objection was not made legal by the United States government until near the end of World War I, with the Selective Service Act of 1917. The Act provided "a member of any well-recognized religious sect or organization," at the discretion of the local Selective Service board, an exemption to combatant service. A person so recognized would only be required to perform duties "declared by the President to be noncombatant." Noncombatant service (eventually classified "1-A-O" by the Selective Service) was the first form of objection officially recognized. Absolute pacifism, the rejection of armed service itself, was not formalized at that time.

"Conscientious objector" was a phrase used derogatorily throughout the 1920s and 1930s to describe those who refused even noncombatant service. Many absolute pacifists suffered under punitive imprisonment that included confinement and abuse so severe as to cause the deaths of at least two Hutterite Anabaptist brothers, Joseph and Michael Hofer. However, public outcry fueled legislation to protect the rights of those who opposed not simply war but military service as an extension thereof. In the event of a draft, many of the same religious groups that were the basis for the original draft of the Second Amendment were crucial to the formation of Civilian Public Service (CPS), which provided the newly legalized objectors a means of witnessing to their devotion to country without having to kill or wear the military uniform. Forms of objection remained diverse, however, and even some pacific religious groups still allowed for national service while remaining critical of lethal force.

A World War II medic named Desmond Doss, a Seventh Day Adventist, refused to carry, clean or train with a rifle, or work at all on Saturdays. The "Prayin' Adventist," as he became known, saved the lives of seventy-five members of his unit (many of whom had made physical threats against him for refusing to bear arms), earning himself a Congressional Medal of Honor. In interviews following his

courageous feat, he insisted that he was not a "conscientious objector," saying the term implied the kind of idle hands in which the
devil could delight. (In fact, he had left a deferment as a shipyard
worker in order to enlist in the Army.) Instead, he called himself a
"conscientious participant," preferring a term that more adequately
described his desire to serve his country as well as his duty to obey
the fifth commandment ("Thou shalt not kill"). His participation
would be dependent upon his conscience, not just his citizenship.

Today, conscientious objection, as recognized by the Supreme
Court (*Gillette v. United States*, 1971), includes only that form of pacifism that objects to all war in any form. Noncombatant status is restricted to chaplains, a specialty that only commissioned officers
may hold, and not enlisted personnel. Even field medics (historically
a place where patriot pacifists could, and did, serve honorably—two
Vietnam conscientious participants were awarded Medals of Honor)
may be required by their unit commander to carry a firearm. In many
units, every military occupational specialty, from cook to x-ray tech-
nician, is trained to be "an infantryman first." It is troubling, however,
given that the primary mission of the Army is not merely war-fighting
but "preserving peace and security." (The fourth and final mission
outlined by Title 10 of the U.S. Code talks about "overcoming nations
responsible for aggressive acts," but even that language points back
to peace and security.)

For just warriors, conscientious participation in particular wars in
response to conscience or the guidance of religious communities
(known, frustratingly, as "selective conscientious objection") is not
at this time legal in the United States. The primary reason for this is
that government bodies have not discerned a method by which the
difference between conscience and cowardice can be differentiated—
how do they know if you genuinely object to a war and do not simply
fear the dangers of the battlefield? Furthermore, pacific scruples
relying too heavily upon political or partisan reasoning could un-
dermine the political authority the nation-state is ordained with
regulating.

Any and every form of just war, however, shares with pacifism an interest in restraining war or preserving justice. Just war and pacifism are very similar in this regard, and neither should be dismissed out of hand. Each of these moral frameworks relies on an informed conscience to make faithful but responsible choices regarding the use of violence. Focused academic interest in conscience is relatively sparse, but the concept evokes significant moral imagery. It is our conscience within which God speaks to every believer; it is that soft, still whisper that moves us toward the good and away from evil. Surrounded by cacophonous trivialities and vocal but ideologically polarized voices from every square, it is to our conscience that we must turn.

The problem with the phrase "conscientious objection" is in its apparent assumption that war is an inevitable, normative expression between states. This names the inherent human reluctance to commit violence as an aberration, an "objection" to the norm. Ironically, through American history, the burden of proof was transferred over time from the government (to make a legitimate case for wars) to individuals, who then had to prove their otherwise natural inclination to live peaceably. In a country founded on individual rights and government obligation, things flipped, individual obligations arose from a perceived right the government had to wage war. The tail wagged the dog.

Further Reading

Bell, Daniel. *Just War as Christian Discipleship: Recentering the Tradition in the Church Rather Than the State*. Grand Rapids: Brazos, 2009.

Boyle, Beth. *Words of Conscience: Religious Statements on Conscientious Objection*. National Inter-Religious Service Board for Conscientious Objectors, 1983.

Clemens, Samuel. "The War Prayer." *Harper's Monthly* (November 1916).

Foster, Gregory D. "Selective Conscientious Objection." *Society* 46, no. 5 (July 8, 2009): 390-93.

Gales and Seaton's History, Annals of Congress. House of Representatives, First Congress, First Session, p. 778. Available at <http://memory.loc.gov/cgi-bin/ampage>.

Journal of the Senate of the United States of America, vol. 1, pp. 63-64. Available at <http://rs6.loc.gov/cgi-bin/ampage>.

Malament, David. "Selective Conscientious Objection and Gillette Decision." *Philosophy and Public Affairs* 1, no. 4 (July 1, 1972): 363-86.

Schlissel, Lillian. *Conscience in America: A Documentary History of Conscientious Objection in America, 1757-1967.* New York: E. P. Dutton, 1968.

Ramsey, Paul. *The Just War: Force & Political Responsibility.* New York: Rowman & Littlefield, 2002.

United States Council of Catholic Bishops. *Catechism of the Roman Catholic Church.* New York: Image, 1995.

Walzer, Michael. *Just and Unjust Wars: A Moral Argument with Historical Illustrations.* Boston: Basic, 2003.

Yoder, John Howard. *When War Is Unjust: Being Honest in Just-War Thinking.* Eugene, Ore.: Wipf & Stock, 2001.

Appendix B

Soldiers in
the New Testament

★

IN EXPLORING THE BIBLICAL ISSUES I've encountered in my journey, I
have been excited to find that soldiers and veterans come to the Bible
with a unique perspective. Here you will find the passages that incor-
porate the Greek words frequently translated "centurion": *hekaton-
tarches* (commander [*tarches*] of one hundred [*hekaton*] men) and
stratiotes (common soldier, from *stratia*—an army.)

Taking notice of these texts will be helpful in discerning what role
soldiers play in the New Testament and what word they might speak
to contemporary centurions. I hope you will find these passages as
challenging and encouraging as I have.

Matthew
8:5-13—the centurion of great faith
27:27-31—soldiers mock Jesus
27:45-54—witness to the crucifixion, culminating in confession
28:11-15—the guards' report

Mark
15:16-20—soldiers mock Jesus

15:33-39—witness to the crucifixion, culminating in confession
15:44-45—burial of Jesus

Luke
3:14—soldiers at the river Jordan
7:1-10—the centurion of great faith
23:11—soldiers mock and dress Jesus in elegant robes
23:26-47—witness to the crucifixion
23:47—confession of the centurion at the cross

John
18:3—soldiers help arrest Jesus
18:12—Jesus' arrest
19:1-37—Jesus' crucifixion orchestrated by soldiers

Acts
10:1-35—Peter and Cornelius the centurion
12:4, 6, 18—Peter's miraculous escape from prison
21:32-35—soldiers protecting Paul
22:25-26—Paul about to be flogged
23:17-18, 23, 31—the plot to kill Paul
24:23—Felix ordering a centurion to watch Paul
27:1, 6, 11, 31-32, 42-43—the storm at sea (centurion named Julius)
28:16—Paul living with a solider to guard him

Epistles
1 Corinthians 9:7
Philippians 2:25
2 Timothy 2:3-4
Philemon 2

Appendix C

Theological Reflections on Military Service

✦

IN THE FIVE YEARS OR SO THAT I have been engaging in conversations about faith and service, there have been a number of questions that get asked over and over again, as well as others that are important but don't get asked openly (some for good reason). In this appendix I hope to address those questions that might have been burning in the back of your mind as you read.

People who ask these questions mostly fall into two groups: (1) those who are themselves serving or have served and (2) those who have close loved ones in the military. However, I think most, if not all, of the commentary below is relevant to anyone with interest in such diverse fields as military and political science, sociology, moral or pastoral theology, mental health and many others.

Those who have family in the service who have reached out to Centurion's Guild have more often than not also been pacifists, so ideology is in play, but ultimately theirs are questions about loving people despite their ideas for or against armed service. There are a lot of great resources for learning more about post-deployment interactions generally, but few of them take into account political or religious differences. I try to include that dynamic here as well.

Because the following have come to me as questions, recreating them here in that same form made sense. I'll address fellow service members in the first section, followed by reflections for family and loved ones. There are many more questions that could (and need to) be asked; to search for or suggest others, go to www.centurionsguild.org.

FOR SERVICE MEMBERS

Don't we need Christians to be a force for good, especially in war?

- There is definitely a case to be made about the need to take war seriously as a moral task, but too often Christians have failed in precisely that task. The most glaring example has been World War II: a Catholic priest blessed the flight crew that dropped the nuclear bombs on Nagasaki, and Ground Zero was the center of Christianity in Japan (Urakami Cathedral, the largest Catholic church in East Asia at the time). My worry is that without a healthy suspicion of war as a prior assumption, any "force for good" is good for nothing. It seems the more important question is not of necessity, but of capacity: *can* Christians be a force for good within the military? If so, selective conscientious objection would have to be guarenteed so that just warriors could serve faithfully and responsibly.

What about war in the Old Testament?

- This is an ongoing and intriguing debate in scholarly circles as well as lay Christian communities. My own reading leaves me with the impression that what we think of as war is very different from what we read about in the Old Testament. (When was the last time a commander ordered his unit to circle a village and blow horns like Joshua did at Jericho?) There seems to be a fundamental difference between contemporary combat and ancient warfare. In the Bible, Israel acted liturgically; they were not obeying God in revenge or in defense of some national self-interest. If it is not a question of replicating what we read about (like inviting the brass section of the Army Band to Fallujah), I'm not sure the question of violence in the Old Testament is easily translatable to our modern understanding of international conflict. Deuteronomy 20 is one of the places that calls for violence, but only after newlyweds, gardeners, new home-owners and cowards (those who are "afraid or faint-hearted"—v. 8) are all dismissed. That doesn't seem very practical. I am a strong advocate of the primacy of Scripture, but there is more to interpreting God's Word than mere translation.

Doesn't God ordain the government to wield the sword?

• I am in general agreement with the "ordained" purpose of government, but of greater importance is what happens when the ordained thing acts in violation of its nature. For example, if an ordained pastor abuses members of our congregation, shouldn't we seriously consider how much trust we place in that person? Ordination is not a license to do whatever one wants; it is a relationship established by God for the furtherance of God's kingdom on earth. Romans 13:1 is no more a blank check for war than Ephesians 5:22 is a license to domestic abuse. The government only retains its God-given authority insofar as it promotes peace.

How do we respond to evil, if not by armed force?

• One of the most underestimated forces for good at our disposal is our own imagination. I always have wondered if we ever would be able to meet the just war criteria of "last resort" if we had more faith in God's ability to inspire us. I don't want to underplay the importance of responding to evil in any way, but I also don't want to encourage the kind of fatalistic assumptions that lead us to think that war is a "necessary evil." Paul warned the Roman church against thinking that evil is required to do good. In fact, he called for their condemnation (Romans 3:8). With Christ's help, we overcome evil not with evil but with good, and I am simply not willing to call war "good."

What about chaplains—is their faith compromised by their military service?

- I think the military is a place of incredible spiritual need. Soldiers deserve every bit as much pastoral care as anyone, and I have spoken to a number of people who are considering military chaplaincy. When I do, however, I remind them that often the most difficult part is trying to differentiate between their allegiance to their country and their faith in God. When you draw a paycheck from the government, it makes it difficult when you are called to bark at the hand that feeds you. There will be times when chaplains' faith calls them to things that their country may not appreciate, but their faith must always trump their national identity. Essentially, their job security should be their lowest priority. I have seen great chaplains and not-so-great chaplains (I was blessed to have been assigned a great chaplain), and the difference has seemed to me to rest on their ability to be honest when national interests get called into question. A great chaplain helps those in their care to seek and know God, regardless of circumstance. A not-so-great chaplain amounts to little more than a government employee.

Should I feel guilty about wanting to enlist?

- The military seems to have a kind of monopoly on the language of sacrifice, honor and obedience, among other virtues. In contrast the church, to many young people I have spoken with, is the place you go when you want to clap your hands for Jesus. Of course, churches rarely have a billion-dollar recruiting budget, but that's another story. Because I think there are profound and important lessons one may learn from military service, and because there is some level of financial security therein, I do not like the discussions about "counter-recruitment," or attempts to prevent military recruitment. Instead, I think people considering enlisting need something more like "recruitment counseling," which would simply offer a counter-narrative to the story a recruiter will give them. I strongly believe that trusting young people enough to help them make their own informed decisions is key. They deserve that much, and when done well, no matter what they decide, that decision is fully their own, one they can own and not doubt or regret.

Is conscientious objection the best way to authentically live out my faith as a Christian?

- Objection is one way to live faithfully as a Christian at a time of war, but it is not the only one. In fact, I think the stark difference that our culture assumes is misleading—there is an entire spectrum between objection and obedience that such an assumption ignores. Just warriors are not always obedient, and objectors are not always pacifists. What I have found helpful is the language of "threshold": Christians must search their conscience for what they feel ultimately violates their moral integrity. For me, that was carrying a weapon. I still had a pocket knife because I never knew when I needed to cut a rope or cut through a juicy steak, but guns aren't good for much other than putting holes in things, like hearts and heads. For some, the threshold might be wearing a uniform or saluting a flag or pledging allegiance to a nation. The Christian life is inherently a moral life, and to lead it well takes reflection, prayer and community feedback. Search your conscience, read your Bible, talk to fellow Christians (just warriors *and* pacifists). Most importantly, seek God: hear and obey that quiet voice of conscience inside you. That's how you live an authentic faith.

I do not feel called to pacifism, but can I object to a war that my church or my conscience deems unjust?

- At this time, a soldier does not have a protected right to exercise her or his conscience. I cover this in more detail in appendix A. Though I consider myself a pacifist, I have great sympathy for those who do not feel the same way as I do about war. Just warriors

are in a tough position because they are, to an extent, illegal; conscience is only formally recognized if it leads one to a kind of absolute pacifism. Men and women are recruited in the United States
at a period in their lives before they are able to develop a solid
moral character; they often don't know what they believe about
war when they sign their enlistment contract. As they mature and
gain life experience—experience that may lead them toward a
kind of contingent pacifism (which allows for the use of organized
violence in some circumstances)—federal law requires that they
choose either "objection to war in *any* form" or obedience to orders
that sometimes are legally or morally ambiguous. This conundrum
is one that must be addressed, especially in a country that insists
that religious expression (including adherence to just war criteria)
is a fundamental and irrevocable civil right.

*Is it possible to love my country's enemies and remain loyal to my country
at the same time?*

• Love is too often misunderstood as accommodating and senti-
  mental. If I love someone, it does not mean they will only ever get
  a pat on the back from me with a smile and a nod. Sometimes
  people I love do wrong, and my love for them requires that I be
  honest and call them out. To love my country is not to always
  agree, to give my "Yes and Amen" to any and all things it does or
  believes. One of my favorite quotes from Dr. Martin Luther King
  Jr. was about how his deep disappointment with America came
  right out of his deep love for his country. Love for one's country is
  found in our admiration as well as our admonition. My country's
  enemies are not my enemies, particularly as a Christian. I embrace
  my enemies, even if my country calls for me to eviscerate them. At
  the heart of this question is another one: Can a nation love its enemies, and, if not, can I still love my country despite that fact?

*I feel as though my military service has made me a part of things that
distance me from God. Can I ever go back to church?*

- We all do evil sometimes, but nobody is beyond redemption. Sin is sin, and there isn't anything that is capable of indefinitely separating you from our Creator. Healing comes to the broken places first, so there is no reason to feel ashamed before God. Find someone you can trust, a battle buddy, someone who can share some of what you're carrying. Maybe that's your pastor, but maybe not. You need to unpack your "hurt locker" with a person or community that will help you digest it all in a healthy and honest way. The essence of church is communion with fellow sinners, and the road to recovery begins with confession. Everything along the way is fellowship, and the road is paved with redemption.

Further Reading

McDonald, Patricia. *God & Violence: Biblical Resources for Living in a Small World*. Harrisonburg, Va.: Herald, 2004.

Tolstoy, Leo. *The Kingdom of God Is Within You*. Lincoln: University of Nebraska Press, 1984.

Trocmé, André. *Jesus and The Nonviolent Revolution*. Maryknoll, N.Y.: Orbis, 2004. Available for free download at <www.plough.com/ebooks/nonviolent revolution.html>.

Wink, Walter. *Jesus and Nonviolence: A Third Way*. Minneapolis: Fortress, 2003.

Yoder, John Howard. *The Christian Witness to the State*. Harrisonburg, Va.: Herald, 2002.

———. *The Politics of Jesus*. Grand Rapids: Eerdmans, 1994.

FOR COMMUNITIES

Someone I love is enlisting or pursuing a commission, but I am not convinced that military service is compatible with Christian faith. What can I do to be true to my convictions while still honoring their service?

- The military is not homogenous; there are a lot of jobs that service members perform that look no different from their civilian counterparts. Combat arms jobs command a lot of our attention, but the great majority of occupations in the Armed Forces are supporting roles. Civilians support combatants as well, even if they aren't in uniform, so I think the sharp contrast between our modern military forces and non-military members of a representative democracy is not so easily made. But more important, even if you disagree strongly about war, I hope that your love for that person is not contingent on their agreeing with you. People we love don't always do what we'd like, but that just gives us the opportunity to learn to love more deeply and in spite of our differences.

A member of my community is getting ready to go to war; are there things I should or shouldn't say?

- Anything you can say that makes it clear to them that you care for them and are ready to do everything you can to support their safe return is a pretty good bet. One thing I think we too often do is to leave our morality up to politics. We don't question war very well, and that leaves those who conduct war with a very weak moral framework through which to interpret what they are going to undertake. Nobody should go to war "because the government says so," but because it is what someone firmly believes will restore peace. Remind them that you know they will do the right thing despite any past mistakes, but that even if mistakes are made you will still love them. Reinforce in whatever way you can that they are a good person and that they will conduct themselves justly and with restraint and concern for the rules of engagement and just war principles.

Has my combat veteran friend killed someone? They won't tell me . . .

- You shouldn't ask. Just get it out of your head entirely. That question makes people uncomfortable for good reason. Is it any less exposing to ask your friend about their favorite sexual position? Let all such questions remain between that person and God. Don't let your morbid curiosity get in the way of asking more meaningful and important questions such as "How are you?" or "Is there anything I can do to support you?" Your job is to create a space within which that experience can emerge naturally and healthfully. If and when that time comes (and it very well might not), you should be prepared to listen to and absorb what they have to share in a non-judgmental, caring and compassionate manner.

Is it wrong to have an American flag in our church or celebrate the military for what good it accomplishes?

• God is the God over all nations, so I am reluctant to suggest that flags have absolutely no place in churches, especially if the flag is displayed in clear subordination to the cross. The problem comes when the flag occupies a liturgical place in worship or community life, or when national liturgies (like national anthems or pledges of allegiance) occur in a church. Church is a unique and holy ("set apart") place that has a different set of values. Instead of having a flag by the pulpit, consider placing it in the entryway or something, not in the same place as the cross or the altar. As for the military, I think we often generically pile everything a military does into our celebration, including killing our enemies. But war is the kind of stuff Christians always mourn, not celebrate. There are some things about the military I agree deserve recognition, like the sacrifice individuals stand ready to make and the discipline they learn, the baby we do not want to toss out with the bathwater of violence and nationalism. But we would do well to recognize other spheres where sacrifice occurs and is equally valid, like education, parenting, medical care—heck, even pastoring, to name a few.

Someone in my congregation is returning from combat. How can I cultivate their participation in our common life?

• For starters, look into your tradition and find the places in which soldiers and centurions appear in liturgy, song and Scripture. For example, in the Roman Catholic Church, the very last thing the congregation says before the priest consumes Holy Eucharist quotes directly from the centurion in Matthew 8. It is amazing where you will find these kinds of things. My experience has been that when soldiers and veterans recognize their presence within the stories, the faith that we all share draws them out of their shell. If you need a primer on preaching texts or scriptural starting points, appendix B has some places you will find soldiers in the New Testament. Furthermore, seek veterans out—do not make them seek you out. Don't require that they identify themselves by asking them to stand up (some are profoundly conflicted about what they've experienced and do not wish to be identified). Rather, go through your congregation and ask people if they know who has military service. Then, find those folks and ask what their unique needs are and how you can minister to them more holistically.

A student I know has been on a deployment. Is the classroom a safe place for them to share their unique insight?

- Knowledge is best gained by experience, and it is impossible to "understand" people in the abstract, without relationship. One thing that our military personnel bring to the classroom is their unique understanding of the Armed Forces and conflict. Those experiences cannot be processed when a veteran or service member is left alone to deal with all that in their own head. One way to alleviate that is to make a space in classrooms to have such experiences discussed considerately and have it diffused within the context of an academic community. Intellectualizing it won't solve the issue, but it is a good start that gives the service member a wider perspective. What this can possibly do is to take them out of their own head by submitting their experiences to the collective conscience. The benefit of all this is to de-abstract war for students and faculty who may not have as immediate of a connection thereto, cultivating a deeper understanding of the violence done in our name—a win-win.

Further Reading

Grossman, Dave. *On Killing*. New York: Back Bay, 2009.
Hedges, Chris. *War Is a Force That Gives Us Meaning*. New York: Anchor, 2003.

Kilner, Pete. "A Moral Justification for Killing in War." *Army Magazine,* February 2010.

Shay, Jonathan. *Achilles in Vietnam: Combat Trauma and the Undoing of Character.* New York: Simon & Schuster, 1995.

———. *Odysseus in America: Combat Trials and the Trials of Homecoming.* New York: Scribner, 2003.

Sherman, Nancy. *The Untold War.* New York: W. W. Norton, 2011.

Thompson, David A., and Darlene Wetterstrom. *Beyond the Yellow Ribbon.* Nashville: Abingdon, 2009.

Tick, Edward. *War and the Soul: Healing our Nation's Veterans from PTSD.* Wheaton, Ill.: Quest, 2005.

Verkamp, Bernard. *The Moral Treatment of Returning Warriors in Early Medieval and Modern Times.* Scranton, Penn.: University of Scranton Press, 2006.

Appendix D

Conscientious Objector Application

★

My June 2006 application for status as a noncombatant conscientious objector is an important artifact of my journey out of the military as a Christian pacifist. When I was going through the procedure, I didn't have many examples of what constituted an adequate packet. I was so used to following examples, I felt more stressed because it felt like I was forging into totally unknown territory. I don't want that to be the case for others discerning between objection and obedience.

By including my original unrevised packet, my hopes are twofold. First, I hope that by seeing what a packet looks like, others considering objector status have some level of stress reduced. Second, it might display a bit more of my character at the time I was applying. It's important to note, however, that half a decade has passed since writing it; hopefully I have matured theologically as well as personally. Reading it over again, there is so much I want to update or just plain delete, but I also want to be honest about the person I was at the time I wrote the following application.

To avoid confusion, I should also point out that what I have included is not by any means everything the regulations require. I have omitted my responses to the thirteen questions in section A (of appendix B, Army Regulation 600-43) since I felt my responses would unnecessarily expose personally identifying information. Section B is made up of questions that outline one's beliefs, when and why they changed, and how they conflict with armed service. Finally, section D asks for references, so I omitted them for the same reasons I omitted my responses to section A. Everything from the regulation is italicized and drawn verbatim from the official regulation, dated August 21, 2006.

This is also an *Army* application; other branches have slight variations on what is required (see the list below for the titles of each branch regulation). All the branches are generally similar, since there is a Department of Defense (DoD) regulation to which they all are subordinate. The GI Rights Network (http://girightshotline.org/en) does an excellent job of outlining the process no matter what branch a client might be from. You can download the latest of each branch regulation, as well as find commentary and context for the discernment process.

If you want to search online for the regulations governing conscientious objection by branch, here are their full titles:

- DoD Instruction 1300.06 "Conscientious Objectors"

- Army Regulation (AR) 600-43 "Conscientious Objection"

- Air Force Instruction (AFI) 36-3204 "Procedures for Applying as a Conscientious Objector"

- Navy MILPERSMAN 15560D, Section 1900-020 "Convenience of the Government Separation Based on Conscientious Objection"

- Marine Corps Order (MCO) 1306.16E "Conscientious Objectors"

- Coast Guard Commandant Instruction (COMDTINST) 1900.8 "Conscientious Objectors and the Requirement to Bear Arms"

✫ ✫ ✫

a. General Information

1. Full name.

2. Social security number.

3. Selective Service number (if applicable).

4. Service address and component (Regular Army [RA], USAR, ARNG).

5. Permanent home address.

6. Name and address of each school and college attended together with dates of attendance, and the type of school (public, church, military, commercial and so forth).

7. A chronological list of all occupations, positions, jobs or types of work, other than as a student in school or college, whether for monetary compensation or not. Include the type of work, name of employer, address of employer, and the from and to date for each position or job held.

8. All former addresses and dates of residence at those addresses.

9. Parent's names and addresses. Indicate whether they are living or deceased.

10. The religious denomination or sect of both parents.

11. Was application made to the Selective Service System (local board) for classification as a conscientious objector before entry into the Armed Forces? If so, to which local board? What decision, if any, that was made by the board, if known?

12. Was any previous application made in service for classification as a conscientious objector? If so, for which status (1–0 or 1–A–O)? Where and when was application made? What was the final determination? Attach a copy of the previous application(s), if any.

13. *When the person has served less than 180 days in the Armed Forces, a statement by him or her as to whether he or she is willing to perform work under the Selective Service civilian work program for conscientious objectors if discharged as a conscientious objector. Also, a statement of the applicant as to whether he or she consents to the issuance of an order for such work by his or her local Selective Service board.*

b. *Training and Beliefs*

1. *An express, specific statement as to whether the person requests classification as a conscientious objector (1–0), or as a conscientious objector (1–A–0):* I am requesting classification as a conscientious objector 1-A-0

2. *A description of the nature of the belief that requires the person to seek separation from the military service or assignment to noncombatant training and duty for reasons of conscience:* I am opposed to participation in combatant training and service because I believe that all life is sacred, that no single human life is worth more or less than any other. I am opposed to violent forms of military force, and the bearing of arms against others, including training myself or others in the use of weapons or munitions. War is wrong, and contributes to the degradation of both the oppressor and the oppressed. In the Old Testament, Yahweh used war to punish sin and protect his people. As a Christian, I believe the Old Testament is a history of God's people, describing his works through man, while the New Testament is the fulfillment of God's plan for atonement, containing the divine word of God, through Jesus. Within the Old Testament he was preparing the Israelites for the coming of our Messiah. Once the Son came to earth, to bring a new era to humanity, war and killing became obsolete; all mankind is now God's chosen people. The payment for sin was death, but Jesus Christ himself paid the ransom for all of us, leaving death as atonement for sin obsolete; anyone who delivers death, then, takes the sac-

rifice that Jesus made on the cross for that person from him. Judgment is God's task and his alone; for me to render death, which is the punishment for sin, would be no less than to usurp that power from the Godhead himself (Romans 12:19). Additionally, to harm any human being would be to inflict that same wound on Jesus himself, as it is written in Matthew 25:40, 45. God's chosen people (all of mankind) are no longer called upon to judge the sins of others through death and destruction. Instead of committing atrocious acts against our brothers, we are to bless those who curse us and pray for those who persecute us, as Jesus did and urges me to do. Modern violence as a means of solving a problem is fruitless, and I feel any less than complete, wholehearted rejection of violence and its principles are required of me to be a follower of Jesus of Nazareth—the humble, loving, self-sacrificing Son of God. Additionally, my conscience and plain reason stand in the way of me taking another person's life, as well as the message of peace the Gospels teach. As the reformer Martin Luther said; "my conscience is captive to the word of God" ["Testimony Before the Diet of Worms," 1521]. I have learned that the unconditional love that the New Testament describes applies to everyone; your neighbor and your enemy (Luke 6:27-28, 35; Matthew 5:44-45), and in no way can loving them be confused with killing them. I value all human life; skin color and nationality have lost their exclusiveness. Ethiopian, Kurd, Jewish, Latino, South African, American, Christian, Chinese, Iraqi, Russian, Muslim, Afghani, Dutch: all of these titles have equal significance to me now—they are all just like me, human. As for serving in the military, there is no difference between a person in a green, grey or blue uniform and any other human being. I wish to continue to love my brothers in the Army even if they choose to act in ways I do not support. In that sense I am not supporting the war, I am supporting them. When they need reassurance, hope, compassion, strength and caring, my hope is that Jesus

Christ can use me to supply them with that (Isaiah 6:8). I hope to be an example of Christ's infinite love, as it is meant even for those who reject it. Love is the overriding message of the entire Bible; the word occurs approximately 584 times. God's agreement with man is referred to as a "covenant of peace" throughout the Old Testament (Numbers 25:12; Isaiah 54:10; Ezekiel 34:25; 37:26; Malachi 2:5). God has put it on my heart to be what Dr. Martin Luther King Jr. called "an extremist for Love" ["Letter from a Birmingham Jail," 1963].

3. *An explanation as to how his or her beliefs changed or developed, to include an explanation as to what factors (how, when, and from whom or from what source training received and belief acquired) caused the change in or development of conscientious objection beliefs:* During my participation in Operation Iraqi Freedom 2, I found it incredibly difficult to suppress emotions I was conditioned to ignore. My feelings toward what I was asked to do would not be quieted. I recognized that the people around me were simply reacting in the way they thought was necessary to "be a good soldier." I was fortunate with how little bloodshed I actually encountered, and even when I did, the horror was pacified by the degrees of separation I was taught—that they were faceless "enemies" or "insurgents." I was surprised when I finally was struck by human suffering in a vehicle rollover near the end of my tour. A cargo [Humvee] full of personnel rolled over a fifteen-foot embankment. My platoon was called to assist in the recovery, and we were the first to arrive. Of all twelve people that were in the vehicle, only one did not survive. [He] was on his right side facing the front [of the Humvee], lying perpendicular to the vehicle, on the edge of a small water reservoir. I thought I was the only one who noticed him, as all the medics shrugged the pair of boots off as not important. My main focus, once my attention was on the injured specialist, was to get one of the several people, including medics, to help me try to remove him from

the wreckage (as all the effort was focused on the victims who were conscious). Nobody would come to his rescue. An hour later, as SF Medics arrived, they finally lifted the vehicle by a crane and pried his limp body from the wreckage. Miraculously, they found a pulse and tried to revive him, just as my platoon was released to return to our Forward Operating Base. I later learned he died on the way to the hospital. That meant he was alive the entire time I was trying to raise attention among those around me. I didn't sleep for two weeks thereafter. It was this that made me realize that the degrees of separation all militaries indoctrinate into their soldiers are a farce. Human life is human life. When I returned from Iraq, I dealt with the PTSD and moved past the guilt. In May of last year, I met an enormously influential family that taught me many things about God's love for his children, and how it is infinite and unconditional. He loves you despite everything, even if you reject him. Not only did they teach it; they lived it. Their awesome example led me to study the Bible for the first time in years; until I was about five or six I went to an Episcopal church, after they prayed that I might not die at three weeks of age from a bout of infantile bronchitis. Because of my newfound interest in the Bible, I decided to enroll in a New Testament history class from Wayland Baptist University. As a result of this class, I began to understand what Christ taught his followers. As time progressed, I began reading more and more biblical resources and books on Protestant theology; to this day I have shelves and shelves of books I couldn't resist picking up, but couldn't wait to finish before I started another one. My views evolved; I went from being pro-choice, to pro-life with a few exceptions, to simply pro-life. My views toward women evolved; I began to understand roles, that women and men were not totally equal (legally and civically they are), but were meant to complement one another physically, spiritually and emotionally in awesome ways, like two unique puzzle pieces. Additionally, I came to an understanding of what Jesus called his followers to do: follow him. I was no longer allowed to be just a believer, but I was to enact everything which I had come to understand. I began to apply that to my occupation in the Army as well. I reflected on what I had experienced in OIF 2 and tried to find a resolution. I realized quickly that I could not compromise my religious convictions. I reached a point where I realized I was serving two masters. My arms are not big enough to carry the sword and the cross. Anything less than complete devotion to his Word would be as if I reject it all. I was to cut the umbilical cord to the old me.

4. *An explanation as to when these beliefs became incompatible with military service and why:* It was in early April that I stumbled upon a friend of mine with whom I had briefly fallen out of touch. He told me he had applied for Conscientious Objector status. I did not realize Conscientious Objectors existed inside the military; I thought it was only for the draft. The most useful tool he gave me was the number of the Army Regulation covering Conscientious Objectors. I initially thought it wasn't for me, but the more I researched it and other sources, I remembered how my arms were stretched between two masters. I began to seriously contemplate my beliefs; I studied both pacifists and supporters of just war theory. After reading several sources, most notably Mark Twain's "The War Prayer," I found that I do not believe there is such a thing as just war, under any circumstances. The Bible reminds us that there is no authority on earth independent from God. Naturally, no governing body may use authority outside God's providence, which has been clearly defined by Jesus, who is God, for such authority would have no foundation. All true authority rests, therefore, on Jesus and his message of love for all mankind. I cannot be coerced by a governing body into contradicting the Word of God, for they would be acting outside the authority of God. Leo Tolstoy wrote "A Christian cannot surrender his

conscience into the will of another man, no matter by what title he may be called" ["Notes for Soldiers," 1901]. On judgment day, I will be weighed based on everything in this life, including actions I took that I was conscientiously opposed to but carried out despite my convictions. My allegiance must rest ultimately with God. I spent several days' worth of time talking to others, reading the AR [Army Regulation] and other written resources. I discussed my plight with many people that have been influential in my life, including secular friends and family, even pastors and religious lay leaders. The most useful thing I did was to pray about it. On April 20, at 9:40 a.m., my prayers were answered. On a bus from Schofield Barracks to HNL, on our way to NTC, I was mulling the issue over in my head while listening to Olivia the Band, a local Christian music group. It was during the fourth track, titled simply "Heaven," when my mind was filled with ideas and thoughts different from my own. My thought pattern had spontaneously gone from "What should I do?" to a soft, compassionate whisper, "here." I was being given the guidance I sought from the one I call Lord. It was ideas, pictures and emotions all in one. I saw myself walking the streets with the confidence of a man who never knew defeat. I knew my assurance came from Christ, and that I was in the Army to love my brothers, be they American, Iraqi, Muslim or secular. I was "touched" by joy; it was such a profound mixture of extreme happiness and assurance, mixed with sadness for knowing how I am still a sinner and need Jesus. I remembered I was once an enemy of God, and I recalled how he waited for me with open arms despite my iniquities. I knew it was the Holy Spirit working to restore me; my heart was broken and I realized where God wanted me. As I was brought to this new realization, I recorded simple thoughts and words onto some receipts I had in my wallet, the only writing material I had on me. Having read the AR, I knew this was what is referred to as "crystallization." It was the need to document my experience for this application that led me to write what little I could. As I wrote down what had occurred and how I felt, I noticed a friend of mine, a devout Catholic (the first person I had told about my moral misgivings about war), was seated behind me. I turned to him, still a little overwhelmed by the experience, and handed him the slips of paper, without a word. He read them all and asked for another piece of paper, on which he wrote (referring to what I had gone through): "Have discerned your own special spiritual vocation from God by extensive prayer and meditation . . . i.e., 'calling.'" I had found my vocation, to remain in the army and provide the light of discipleship to those who may find themselves in a dark world. Dr. Martin Luther King Jr. spoke of this darkness when he wrote about violence from the Birmingham jailhouse: "The ultimate weakness of violence is that it is a descending spiral, begetting the very thing it seeks to destroy. Instead of diminishing evil, it multiplies it . . . adding deeper darkness to a night already devoid of stars." I was immediately faced with the question of when I should inform my superiors of this realization. Over the course of discussing my query with others, I was given numerous quotes from the Bible about obeying the authority of those appointed over you. Most notably Hebrews 13:17, which states in part: "[Have confidence in your leaders] so that their work will be a joy, not a burden, for that would be no benefit to you." (Other great passages are Titus 3:1-2 and 1 Timothy 2:12.) These passages showed me it would not be appropriate to enact this as we headed to the most pivotal training we had planned before our deployment, while stress levels were high and the workload was highly demanding. I would not be asked to kill or harm a single person in training, and I knew there are other facets of my MOS that I could focus on that encouraged survivability, observation and information sharing. Within days of arriving at NTC, I informed a few more people of my feelings toward war, including the chaplain, the battalion Fire Support Sergeant, and my Fire Support Officer. I told them of my intention to respectfully approach my commander and First Sergeant once the two-week training was complete and when we reached an appropriate administrative pause. My wish was to informally bring them up to speed about how I felt. With that information, I hoped to show them that I wished to be open and honest about my religious beliefs, and then formally submit this application upon return to Hawaii. Fortunately, the one private I was entrusted to train knew the training in NTC was not intended in any way to be an encouragement to kill, but to maintain situational awareness and to use our job as a last resort, or to defend the maneuver platoon. I have an enormous amount of respect for him to this day for the understanding he had for how conflicted I was at some points of the training. He knows that I have been called to be a peacemaker, as Jesus spoke of in Matthew 5:9; "Blessed are the peacemakers, for they will be called children of God." Not only is my objection to war a religious conviction; morally and ethically it is wrong as well. Since I was a child I was taught "two wrongs don't make a right." At what point are we, as adults, told that that is no longer valid, yet continue to teach our children a lesson we do not follow ourselves? Violence begets violence, and I cannot continue to contribute to the descending spiral. "Do not repay anyone evil for evil. Be careful to do what is right in the eyes of everybody" (Romans 12:17).

5. *An explanation as to the circumstances, if any, under which the person believes in the use of force, and to what extent, under any foreseeable circumstances:* The use of force which I oppose includes excessive, premeditated violence benefiting one individual or group over another. Military force is wrong because it is detached, indiscriminate violence often perpetuated against innocents. Combatants are often required to remove

themselves from their intellect; as the popular saying goes, they are not "paid to think." As a Christian, I cannot separate myself from my mind or conscience. No war can be free from collateral damage, and war is therefore destructive to people completely free from transgression, or who may even oppose the same ideology the aggressor is attempting to defeat. As an ethical proposal, war can never achieve its intended purpose, and history has shown us that violent overthrow leads to more violent replacement regimes; the French Revolution led to the Reign of Terror, World War II and the Russian Revolution led to the Red Terror and the rise of Stalin, etc. That is the reason I am opposed to revolutionary violence as well, as it is based on the idea of "redemptive violence," that one can solve violence with violence. Jesus didn't overthrow the Romans, as the Jews [of the first century] wished the Messiah to do; he overthrew the power of sin, through His nonviolent sacrifice on the cross. Redemptive violence is self-defeating. Albert Einstein believed "peace cannot be kept by force. It can only be achieved by understanding" ["Notes on Pacifism"]. Acceptable uses of force may include personal self-defense or defense of other oppressed or innocent individuals. Although, in drawing the sword to protect Jesus, the only sinless, innocent man ever to walk the earth, Peter is corrected and told "he that draws the sword shall die by the sword" (Matthew 26:52). Not even the defense of the divine Son of God constituted bloodshed. Acceptable means of force must still appeal to the end of loving another human being, for example, spanking a child. You may be teaching the child a lesson, but you would not spank a child to death, that could never be an appeal to love them. Police force may constitute an acceptable means of using force, since all policemen only act within a specific, assigned area and do not deviate from their jurisdiction. International war does not; it brings fear and persecution to the doorsteps of innocent people. Also, police aim

only to arrest and subdue through non-lethal means, while
military violence lays destructive waste to entire peoples and
villages. War also frequently is conducted outside the limits of
even international law, while police forces must answer for
their deeds and misdeeds. There can be no distinction between killings on a mass scale and killing singularly; both are
equally wrong. I am reminded of the lesson I was taught when
I was a child: "just because everyone else was jumping off the
bridge doesn't make it right." Nonviolence is an ideal which
many people feel is a viable alternative, and it has been proven
successful in the abolition of slavery, the American Civil
Rights Movement and Women's Suffrage in America, even the
liberation of India from Great Britain. I feel nonviolence ex-
emplifies Christ's undying love even for those who crucified
him. Only the most committed, determined followers succeed
in nonviolence. Regardless, I feel it is an objective the Scriptures have steered me toward pursuing.

6. *An explanation as to what in the person's life most conspicuously
   demonstrates the consistency and depth of his or her beliefs that
   have rise to his or her claim:* The traits that I feel demonstrate
   my consistency and depth most are probably my open-mind-
   edness and willingness to discuss with others what I feel is
   the true message of the Gospels. I was never so vocal or confident in my beliefs until I began studying the Bible on a personal level with an open heart. I have lost sleep some nights
   because I want to shout from the rooftops that I am a new
   creation. My eagerness to share the Gospel, or evangelize, is
   apparent to those who know me personally. Also, I now take
   an earnest interest in immersing myself in the Bible and the
   writings of the early Christian fathers. Violent video games
   have lost their allure, as well as horror movies and books. I
   just don't have an interest in them anymore. I have also found
   new music I thought I'd never listen to: Christian rock and
   gospel. I have written to several authors who have inspired

me, and some have written back. They have expressed gratefulness that I am abiding by his commandments and have sought my vocation earnestly and fervently. In order to meet with people across the country who have shown me support, I fought vigorously for a week of leave in late June. In order to see the commander personally about my request for leave, I changed my flights within the block leave period and gave up three days of leave that I was told were already approved. On a professional level, my first Non-Commissioned Officer Evaluation Reprot stated in the remarks that I was willing to stand up for what I thought was right. I have no disciplinary marks on my record, but more than enough professional accomplishments which display both my determination and my dedication to those in service. I also had good practice in turning the other cheek when I was assaulted by a subordinate earlier this year. Had I returned the force, I would have mirrored exactly that which I seek to destroy. Also, since returning from the National Training Center, I have made all the arrangements for interviews and furnished all the agencies with copies of my application. This is clearly assigned to command responsibility in AR 600 43, Chapter 2, Paragraph 2, Line E. Additionally, in mid-May, while deployed to the National Training Center, I wrote an email to all of my friends, family and acquaintances explaining how I had changed dramatically, but wished to remain their friend or family and yet be recognized as radically different. It was a leap of faith, one which I feared might meet with some rejection. The umbilical had to be cut if I was to be reborn. On a deeper level, the development of and adherence to my newfound beliefs has cost me my relationship with my now ex-girlfriend. One of the main reasons she felt we were incompatible was the fact that our beliefs were going in different directions. We had been dating over a year when we went our separate ways. Soon, I hope to be baptized near my home, offering myself as a living sacrifice to God as the baptismal water washes my sins from my soul. Baptism is tied irrevocably to repentance, or turning from sin. A changed life is the outward manifestation of reconciling one's heart to God and becoming his child. To be God's child is to follow in his way. It is for this reason that I can no longer hate and induce fear in my fellow man. For to hate him would be the same as killing him, as 1 John 3:15 reminds us "Anyone who hates his brother is a murderer, and you know that no murderer has eternal life in Him." Matthew 5:21-22a also reminds us that even mere thoughts are as potent as the deeds themselves: "You have heard that it was said to the people long ago, 'Do not murder [Exodus 20:13], and anyone who murders will be subject to judgment.' But I tell you that anyone who is angry with his brother will be subject to judgment." The root of this change lies in my eagerness to show love for my fellow man, that is the critical test of discipleship. God is not interested in destruction, but in redemption.

7. *An explanation as to how the applicant's daily lifestyle has changed as a result of his or her beliefs and what future actions he or she plans to continue to support his or her beliefs:* Jim Wallis reminds us that "The making of peace can result in great conflict . . . it will cost something, and it will often make us misunderstood in a world that knows violence better than peace." However, "Following the way of Jesus into practical peacemaking and nonviolent conflict resolution has become a critical vocation for Christians in a world of violence" [*Call to Conversion*]. In a violent world, the peacemaker has an uphill battle, one which is seemingly endless and without reward. Despite obstacles, one must do what they can to promote peace and offer alternatives to violence, as Jesus calls me to do. While I was in Tennessee, I was asked to speak on my feelings toward war and how I feel peacemakers can contribute to waging peace in response to violence. For three

days in Washington D.C., I lobbied Hawaiian and Californian Senators to make poverty and war issues of utmost importance and relevancy to their political agendas. I approached major religious leaders with ideas for how to tackle issues of war as Christians in a violent world. To other emerging youth in the political arena, I reminded them not to forget the real issues surrounding war and injustice that peacemakers are called to combat. I was interviewed in depth for a documentary about how I believe the Bible addresses the issue of violence both in history and in the world today. In Hawaii, I am preparing to lead a Bible study on biblical war and what bearing that it has on Christians in the modern era. I am an active member of several Christian message boards and forums, both seeking the advice of others and being sought for advice. Besides my offering in church on Sundays, I also tithe at least 10 percent of my total income to a community devoted to developing relationships with the poor and helping to meet their needs both materially and financially. In short, I am quickly learning my calling to be a faith-based social justice and peace activist. I will seek to provide the fruits of the spirit; "love, joy, peace, forbearance, kindness, goodness, faithfulness, gentleness and self-control." As Galatians 5:22-23 says, "there is no law" against such things.

c. Participation in Organizations

1. *Information as to whether the person has ever been a member of any military organization or establishment before entering upon his or her present term of service. If so, the name and address of such organization will be given together with reasons why he or she became a member:*

2. *A statement as to whether the person is a member of a religious sect or organization:*

3. *A description of the applicant's relationships with and activities in*

all organizations with which he or she is or has been affiliated, other than military, political or labor organizations:

d. *References.*
Any more information that the person desires to be considered by the authority reviewing his or her application. Letters of reference or official statements of organizations to which the applicant belongs or refers in his or her application are included. The burden is on the applicant to obtain and forward such information.

Appendix E

Timeline of Events

2000

February 16: Signed enlistment contract with U.S. Army

May: Graduated high school in Santa Ana, California

August 9: Shipped from Los Angeles military entrance station to Ft. Sill, Oklahoma, for initial military training

2001

March: Arrived at Ft. Bragg, North Carolina, for first duty assignment in Charlie Battery, 2-319th Airborne Field Artillery Regiment, 82nd Airborne Division

September 11: At a dental appointment as the World Trade Center towers fell

2002

August 8: Reenlisted for four years and an assignment to Schofield Barracks, Hawaii

December 20: Left Ft. Bragg on interim leave on the way to Hawaii

December 30: Learned my old unit would become part of the initial invasion force into Iraq

2003

January 18: Arrived at my new artillery unit in Hawaii, attached to Bravo Company, 1-14th Infantry Battalion, 2nd Brigade, 25th Infantry Division (Light)

2004

January 19: Departed for Kuwait from Hickam Airfield, Hawaii
February 2: Crossed line of embarkation into Iraq
February 4: First IED attack and nightmare
April 1-14: Battalion became a Quick Reaction Force for Iraq
June 22: Ambush outside Najaf
October 1-15: Fought in Samarrah during Operation Baton Rouge
November 16: Failed rescue mission northwest of Baqubah

2005

January 30: Election Day in Iraq, Iraqi soldier injured by a grenade outside a Mosul safe-house
February 16: Returned to Hawaii
May: Met Thena after post-deployment military ball
June: Began Bible study with Uncle Jimmy, started seriously questioning war
October: Transfered units within 25th Infantry Division

2006

April 16: Easter Sunday
April 20 (Thursday): Vision in the bus on the way to training exercises
April 20-May 20: Pre-deployment training at Ft. Irwin, California
May 23 (Tuesday): Mental Status Evaluation with Dr. Leonard
May 29 (Monday): Chaplain's assessment interview
June 4: Pentecost Sunday
June 5 (Monday): Formal submission of CO packet
June 6 (Tuesday): Pre-deployment leave began: California and Tennessee (PAPA Fest)
June 7 (Wednesday): Broke up with Thena

June 11: Trinity Sunday (First Sunday in Ordinary Time)

June 28 (Wednesday): Returned from leave

July 4 (Thursday): Baptism

July 5 (Friday): Visited with lawyers

July 10 (Monday): Meeting with First Sergeant: "You got what you wanted"

July 13 (Thursday): Meeting with Captain: "Don't ever step foot on my company again"

August: Watched my infantry battalion deploy to Iraq without me

October 19: Began terminal leave period, wrote "Liberty & Justice for All?"

November 20-December 16: Israel/Palestine with Christian Peacemaker Teams

November 21: Formal discharge from active duty

November 30: Hebron experience, wrote "A Journey of Healing in Hebron"

December 3-24: Advent

December 7: Bus experience in Palestine

2007

January 23: Arrived on the East Coast for life in community in Camden, New Jersey

March 16: Liturgist at the Christian Peace Witness for Iraq in Washington, D.C., experience before the fresco of Jesus' resurrection

Acknowledgments

THIS BOOK WOULD NOT HAVE BEEN POSSIBLE without the ceaseless support from my editor, Dave Zimmerman, and my friend, Shane Claiborne. Dave and Shane were each instrumental in the entire process of writing, and they bore with me despite my infinite doubts. This book is as much a product of their commitment as it is my own.

I was fortunate to have a great number of friends revise and refine my writing in innumerable ways. Before the first draft manuscript was even completed, Genevieve Burbridge, Sarah Campbell, Alaina Kleinbeck, Enuma Okoro, Tiffany Prest and Nate Rauh attended a pre-pre-release gathering that would become one of my first lessons in humility regarding my writing abilities. Their gentle but honest criticisms were invaluable to me and increased my confidence (and maybe my writing ability) infinitely. I am especially grateful to John Heuer for the use of his space to write much of the original material.

As the manuscript continued to take shape, more friends helped by commenting directly on my drafts, highlighting key events, pointing out confusing jargon and generally increasing the read-ability of the final version you hold in your hands. A hearty thank you is due to Sara Blaine, Banks Clark, Meghan Florian, Ebony

Grisom, Samuel Gunter, Stanley Hauerwas, Kim Hodges, Sarah Howell, Mary Hulse, David Johnston, Herman Keizer, Pete Kilner, David Mahaffey, Anna Masi, Scott Schomburg, Andy Scott and Isaac Villegas. If I have written coherently at all, it is their tireless energy that should be credited.

One last push was made during Advent 2012 to polish up the last major revision to the manuscript. Katie DeConto, Russell Johnson, Amber Noel, Dave Swanson and Laura Turdie were part of that effort, and their insights were invaluable to the completion of the manuscript.

Finally, men and women who have in common with me not only the martial fraternity but also a deep and abiding sense of Christian service have sustained this literary journey. On numerous occasions, Andrew Bell, Jennifer Blain, Zach Cornelius, Kyle Caldwell, Alan Felton, Joe Gibson, Isaac Simerly and Nate Wildermuth patiently reminded me that I am not the only one crazy enough to believe this stuff. Their encouragement, presence and persistence have helped to keep me grounded.

Notes

✯

Introduction

[1]Abraham Heschel, interview with Carl Stern, "A Conversation with the Late Dr. Abraham Heschel," *NBC News* (aired February 4, 1973). Read the transcript at <www.philosophy-religion.org/religion_links/aj_heschel.htm>.
[2]Abraham Heschel, *The Insecurity of Freedom* (New York: Macmillan, 1966).

Movement One

[1]To this day, my mom continues to work eleven-hour days, six days a week. Every year, her job is threatened because she has no seniority, having given up crucial career-building years to raise four children. The service she performed in the home is not assigned a value in the gross domestic product, but her output may in the end exceed that of some smaller U.N. member nations.
[2]Paul actually does not use *mysterion* for what we call sacraments, though the connection is important. The Latin word *sacramentum,* used in some early texts, comes from *sacer* ("something holy or sacred"). In the Roman world, the *sacramentum* was the sacred oath that conscripts were required to profess before entering military service. Paul conscripted a number of imperial words for service in the church: Jesus, not Caesar, is our *kyrios* (Lord, master); *evangelion* (the good news) announced not Caesar but Jesus. By being baptized, the early Christians were professing an oath not to Caesar and his centurions but to the holy mystery of God and his Son, our Lord, Jesus Christ.

[3]To enter the military, every recruit has to take the Armed Services Vocational Aptitude Battery, or "ASVAB." How they score determines the Military Occupational Specialties (MOS) made available to them, so the better you do, the more options you have. (Not all branches let you choose like the Army does, however.) The more in-demand the job is, and the higher scores that were required, the more money for college a recruit is offered. Therefore, a highly technical, hard-to-fill job gave the most. Though technically a field artillery position, Forward observers are required to have good scores and are highly technical but are assigned to infantry units; the risk (and the demand) is high; therefore the reward (college money) is greater.

[4]Tim O'Brien, *The Things They Carried* (New York: Broadway, 1998), pp. 65-66.

[5]I am sure that I am butchering this highly complex process. To understand operant conditioning and killing in war more reliably, Lieutenant Colonel Dave Grossman's *On Killing* (Boston: Back Bay, 2009) is a of utmost importance. It is a comprehensive and exhaustive account of the psychological process required to kill other human beings in war.

[6]Concrete data on infantry units in regards to suicide, depression, and so on, is lacking right now. However, Lieutenant Colonel Kilner and others are making a very strong case that individual moral decay and reflexive fire are closely related. We do not need more soldiers thinking less; we need more soldiers thinking more: training service members in the moral framework of war-fighting is key, Kilner suggests, to effective and efficient military strategy. *Soldiers of Conscience* won the full support and endorsement of the United States Army and truly is fair and balanced—an indispensable resource for anyone and everyone thinking through morality and military service. Available at <www.soldiers-themovie.com>.

[7]The hardening of Pharaoh's heart is frustratingly debatable. Exodus 7–10 seems to contain an equal number of verses attributing Pharaoh's hardened heart to either God or Pharaoh himself (God did it: Exodus 9:7; 10:1, 20; Pharaoh did it: Exodus 8:15, 32; 9:34). The moral repercussions are daunting; for one, who is at fault for the decimation of the Egyptian Army in Exodus 14—Pharaoh or God? That is another book entirely . . .

[8]A truck bomb was exploded below the north tower of the World Trade Center on February 26, 1993, killing six but failing to bring down the twin towers as planned. The convicted conspirators had ties to Al Qaeda, which would later claim responsibility for the 2001 attacks.

[9]If you want to read more about how the military is organized, a good resource is <www.trailblazersww2.org/history_infantrystructure.htm>.

[10]*The Ground Truth: After the Killing Ends* (Focus Features, 2006). I cannot

recommend the film enough. Learn more at <www.thegroundtruth.net/focusfeatures/film/the_ground_truth>.

[11]Philip Zimbardo, *The Lucifer Effect: Understanding How Good People Turn Evil* (New York: Random House, 2007).

[12]Stanley Milgram, *Obedience to Authority; An Experimental View* (New York: Harper & Row, 1974).

[13]Lieutenant Colonel Grossman (himself an Army Ranger) and his book *On Killing* were cited above (see note 5). The United States Army has actually developed their own video game, called *America's Army,* available as a free download (since "digital download makes it easier than ever"). War, however, is not a game; the great moral work of soldiering is by no means entertaining, nor should it ever be sold as such. *America's Army* has been criticized widely for being used as a both a recruitment tool and a training aid.

[14]Tyler Boudreaux makes a number of allusions to Dante's *Inferno* in his own reflections about combat service in Iraq in *Packing Inferno: The Unmaking of a Marine* (Port Townsend, Wash.: Feral House, 2008).

[15]I probably have an overly simplistic interpretation of *Platoon.* To me, Taylor was a kind of archetypal good guy trying to keep his nose clean in Vietnam, set against the proverbial bad guy displayed through Sergeant Barnes, who has done something wrong and wants to cover it up. I was vaguely troubled when I became aware of an allusion to Jesus in *Platoon's* hero: Chris T.

[16]I am being only slightly figurative here. Many people do in fact look in the mirror and see the emotional toll of combat displayed in their very faces. If you don't believe me, check out one student's art project in the Netherlands, where she took frontal pictures of a number of soldiers before, during and after a deployment to Afghanistan (the significance is in their eyes): <www.clairefelicie.com/category/marked>.

[17]Thrice, "At the Last," *Beggars* (Vagrant, 2009). Thrice's music has been surprisingly therapeutic for me, particularly their *Alchemy Index, Beggars* and *Come All You Weary.* Find them at <www.thrice.net>.

[18]In March 2008, I testified on behalf of Iraq Veterans Against the War <www.ivaw.org> at a conference called Winter Solider: Iraq and Afghanistan, held at the National Labor College in Silver Spring, Maryland. Over seventy people testified, including civilians, experts, military families and military personnel affected by the wars in Iraq and Afghanistan. A book published by the same name (Chicago: Haymarket, 2008) documents much of the painfully honest, verified firsthand accounts. (The recorded testimony is available online at <www.youtube.com/ivaw>.) The model for the event was the 1971 Winter Soldier Investigation convened by Vietnam Veterans Against the War, <www.wintersoldierfilm.com>.

Movement Two

[1]Heschel made these statements repeatedly throughout his speaking and teaching, with only slight variations. You can read them both in the context of his life, described by his daughter Susannah, in her introduction to an edited volume of his essays titled *Moral Grandeur and Spiritual Audacity* (New York: Farrar, Straus, and Giroux, 1997). Prayerful action (or actionable prayer) is a central tenet of my reading of the Gospels and shouldn't be overlooked. I believe strongly in the correlation between faith and action; prayer is a precursor to action, and action can be profoundly prayerful.

[2]The IED was the predominant weapon used against U.S. forces in Iraq, though some suggest that all explosive devices in war are improvisational, since war is by its very nature chaotic. I don't like the term *IED*, since it is only ever really used to describe enemy devices. Would damage caused by nonimprovised explosive devices (like a landmine or artillery shell) be any less deplorable? Anyway, I think the term *IED* is morally confusing unless we're willing to consider our own devices in similar ways and with similar language.

[3]PTSD is one of the major medical diagnoses coming out of Iraq and Afghanistan, but not all service members are seeking treatment. The culture of the military de-incentivizes admitting weakness or injury, but there is a push to destigmatize mental health issues like PTSD.

[4]During my time stationed at Schofield, I only had "LAITURI" on my uniform, as opposed to "MEHLLAITURI," which is how my Army nametape appeared at Ft. Bragg. In a nutshell, the long states and getting called "alphabet" got real boring, real quick. I dropped my mom's maiden name informally and have regretted it ever since. I've used my full name in the body of this book for consistency, though it might throw off the few folks who read this that knew me during that time. I also was known as Lucky (Logan "Lucky" Laituri) in Hawaii, though it fell out of use after I was discharged.

[5]It does mean, however, that we have to put our laptops and tablets down long enough to engage in face-to-face encounters . . .

[6]As cliché as this sounds, it is the only way I can think of to describe the feeling that threatened to envelope me. To illustrate more precisely how grave the situation in Mexico was (or could have been), watch the film *In the Valley of Elah* (Warner, 2007). Based on actual events surrounding the violent death of a young private just returned from Iraq, the final climactic scene illustrates just how easy it is to slide into a kind of moral dementia. Without giving away the plot, it would suffice to say that, that evening in Mexico, I could have very easily have become Corporal Penning.

[7]St. Telemachus's feast day is celebrated every January 1, which in 404 C.E. was the last day that the gladiatorial games took place. Since 1967, the first day of the year has also been known in the Roman Catholic Church as World Peace Day.

[8]"Joe" is an informal way to refer to soldiers of rank E-4 Specialist and below, as in "G.I. Joe." Ted didn't know at the time that I was a sergeant, but it wouldn't have made a difference.

[9]I deployed to Iraq in 2004 with 1-14th Infantry Regiment, 2nd Brigade, 25th Infantry Division (Light). When 2nd Brigade was transformed into a Stryker brigade, many of us went to other units on Oahu. I do not identify the unit I was transferred to in late 2005 in order to protect the privacy of those involved.

[10]A person's "ETS" date, which stands for Expiration Term of [military] Service, is the day their active service ends and their inactive service begins. If active service lasted longer than eight years, then the person has no inactive service required.

[11]I am grateful to LTC Pete Kilner for insisting, during his keynote address at the 2011 After the Yellow Ribbon event at Duke Divinity School, that beauty and tragedy exists simultaneously in war. Organized by student group Milites Christi (Latin: "soldiers of Christ"), After the Yellow Ribbon has produced a number of resources for past and present service members and their families, congregations and local communities <http://sites.duke .edu/aftertheyellowribbon/media/>.

[12]The Orange County Supertones, "Louder Than the Mob," *Supertones Strike Back* (BEC, 1997). I was a huge fan of The Supertones back in the day, so I was pretty excited to hear they semi-reunited in the summer of 2010, <http://supertones.webs.com/>.

[13]Derek Webb, "Intro to 'Nobody Loves Me,'" *The House Show* (INO records, 2004). The quote is within a longer discussion about joy, which is important to highlight. We cannot know joy without understanding the cost at which it comes. We cannot jump for joy without first having our hearts broken by conviction and being moved to contrition. We cannot get to the soft whisper of grace until we are floored by the thunderclap of guilt.

[14]To get the most up-to-date versions of these applications, consult the GI Rights Network, a strictly non-governmental affiliation of organizations who specialize in military counseling. Visit <www.girightshotline.org/en> or make a toll-free, confidential call to them at (877) 447-4487. I also include more information on the various military regulations in appendix D.

[15]Olivia the Band, "Heaven," *Olivia the Band* (Essential Release, 2005). Olivia was a band local to the North Shore, and it was always a pleasure to watch

them play at the gym where I went to church. In fact, the lead singer and I had a really invigorating conversation about faith and service not long after I turned in my CO packet.

[16]The notion that "every man is an infantryman first" is meant partly to reassure military personnel not in combat arms specialties that they were also valued. Combat infantry, or "grunts," were often unofficially thought of as "real soldiers," as opposed to lowly "POGs," or "Personnel Other than Grunt." The effect of declaring that "everyone is an infantryman first," however, was to dismiss the notion that we could serve without a rifle—the infantryman's best friend and lover. In Vietnam there were a small number of jobs in which noncombatants could serve, such as medicine, but that practice has (tragically) fallen out of practice. Currently, even medics may be required by their commanding officer to carry a firearm.

Movement Three

[1]As alarming as it might seem to take protective gear away from a frontline combatant for his or her refusal to kill, it is not without precedent. Aidan Delgado describes being relieved of his Kevlar plates after he applied to be a CO while deployed to Iraq in his book *The Sutras of Abu Ghraib: Notes from a Conscientious Objector in Iraq* (Boston: Beacon, 2007).

[2]For more information about the requirement variances between branches, see appendix D. See also the "Guide for COs in the Military," <www.centeronconscience.org/images/stories/pdf/The_Guide_for_COs_ in_the_Military.pdf>.

[3]Jimmy writes about war packages in his own book *God's Hand in the Life of an Electrician* (Kapolei, Hawaii: White Mountain Castle, 2008).

[4]John Howard Yoder, *What Would You Do?* (Scottdale, Penn.: Herald, 1992). Do please take the time to read it; it will be time very well spent.

[5]Beth Boyle, ed., *Words of Conscience: Religious Statements on Conscientious Objection* (The National Interreligious Service Board for Conscientious Objectors, 1983). "NISBCO" was born in 1940 to protect the rights of religious conscientious objectors. In 1983, NISBCO self-published the tenth edition of *Words of Conscience*. Despite its age, the book is one of the most comprehensive on the market to discuss conscience and war from a religious perspective. Their name change in June 2000 to The Center on Conscience & War reflects their streamlined mission. They are a founding member organization of the GI Rights Network operating out of Washington, D.C., and you can reach them at (202) 483-2220 or online at <www.centeronconscience.org> to get copies of *Words of Conscience*.

[6]The venomous language around COs is something unique to our current

culture and political climate. Until recently, there were more COs than Navy Seals with Medals of Honor. As recently as the Korean War COs served alongside infantrymen as combat medics; COs Thomas Bennett and Joseph LaPointe were both Medal of Honor recipients who were killed in action in Vietnam. Stories of soldier saints and patriot pacifists will inform my next book (forthcoming, Herald Press).

[7]"The War Prayer" was eventually published in *Harper's Monthly* in November 1916, about one year before President Wilson declared war on Germany, and the United States entered World War I.

[8]I am working on a second book, *For God & Country (in that order): Faith and Service for Ordinary Radicals,* that will distill testimonies of soldier saints and patriot pacifists. You might have noticed I include a fair number of them already. Keep an eye out for it in 2013 from Herald Press.

[9]I explain very briefly at the end of appendix A why this phrase is problematic. Essentially, "objection" seems to imply that war (the thing against which I am "objecting") is primary. In contrast, peaceableness is normative, and war the abberation. It might be more accurate to describe just warriors, for example, as "contingent pacifists" (their pacifism, being normative, is contingent upon certain criteria like protection of the innocent, just cause, proportionality, etc.).

[10]Richard Goldstein, "Desmond T. Doss, Heroic War Objector, 87, Dies," *The New York Times,* March 25, 2006, <www.nytimes.com/2006/03/25/national/25doss.html>.

[11]Official World War II historian S. L. A. Marshall first suggested this data in his 1947 book *Men Against Fire: The Problem of Battle Command* (Norman: University of Oklahoma Press, 2000).

[12]Here again is what Dave Grossman describes as operant conditioning in his *On Killing,* mentioned above in movement one, note 4.

[13]One that we could begin with might be "Why, if a 25 percent firing rate resulted in *winning the war,* should we need to change anything?"

[14]I share more about just war criteria in appendix A.

[15]See Acts 5:29.

[16]Read about Maximilian's passion at <www.ucc.ie/milmart/Maximilian.html> and about Marti in Regine Pirnoud, *Martin of Tours* (Boston: Ignatius Press, 2006).

[17]There is actually an entire litany of soldier saints the church has at its disposal that should inform our orientation toward war and peace and statecraft. Centurion's Guild publishes an online calendar of saints and holy people who share in the martial fraternity and who wrestled with what it means to serve God and country (in that order); see <http://bit.ly/A6g1mq>.

[18]You can read the transcription from that speech at <www.american rhetoric.com/speeches/dwightdeisenhowerfarewell.html>.

[19]"GI" refers to an acronym suggesting that soldiers, in their uniformity, are "Government Issued." It doesn't seem as popularly used a phrase as it was a generation ago.

[20]Thomas Jefferson, letter to William S. Smith, November 13, 1787. Compiled by Saul Padover in his book *Jefferson on Democracy* (New York: New American Library, 1954).

[21]Centurion's Guild, a community I describe in movement five, has compiled a list of such men and women on our website, www.centurionsguild.org. We also send out updates on their feast days, a reminder to live our lives in light of what those before us have lived and learned.

[22]The numbers here reflect a basic word search on Accordance for Mac. I found different numbers when I originally did my search, which was frankly not the most accurate method: I basically counted the number of times the *Zondervan NIV Study Bible* listed the word in its concordance. *War* was cited much less and *love* cited much more. The current numbers are still indicative of my basic conclusion: it's about love!

[23]Philip Zimbardo, author of *The Lucifer Effect* (mentioned in movement one, note 11), visited my alma mater (Hawaii Pacific University) while I was still enrolled there. I asked him about how the Lucifer Effect might inform our understanding of the actions that soldiers in combat take, and how social pressure and roleplay created a kind of groupthink situation for military units. Referencing his Heroic Imagination Project (HIP, <http://heroic imagination.org>), he suggested that conscientious objection represented a kind of heroic imagination, especially in the case of incidental objection, such as Hugh Thompson Jr., who put a stop to the My Lai massacre in 1968. He was accused of much worse than cowardice, receiving death threats, hate mail and even mutilated animals on his doorstep, before finally being awarded the highest award the Army offered for actions not involving direct contact with an enemy. Heroes are not made; they emerge. I'm sure that it is for this reason that the Beatitudes end with the promise of blessing for enduring persecution, since it so often comes far after it is due.

[24]Sulpicius Severus wrote *The Life of St. Martin* while the bishop of Tours was still alive. You can now find the text in *The Nicene and Post-Nicene Fathers*, series II, vol. 11, ed. Philip Schaff (Grand Rapids: Hendrickson, 1995), available at <www.ccel.org/ccel/schaff/npnf211/Page_3.html>.

[25]Sebastian was a secret Christian serving as captain in the Praetorian Guard. When the emperor discovered this, he had Sebastian tied to a tree and shot full of arrows. Miraculously, though the archers were fooled, Se-

bastian lived. God can only know why, but this wasn't enough for the saint, who surely startled the emperor when he appeared at a parade before his former commander in chief, berating and taunting him, before the emperor had him beaten to death.

[26]Regulations for the other branches can be found in appendix D.

[27]See <www.papafestival.org/about.htm>. Language like "Celebrate, support, and empower one another" and "foster the development of DIY, earth-sustaining, and relationship-building" is not the type with which I was familiar after about five years of active military service.

[28]Chris Haw has a book coming out about his conversion from nondenominational evangelical Protestant to Roman Catholic. I was privileged to have read early drafts of *From Willow Creek to Sacred Heart* (Notre Dame, Ind.: Ave Maria Press, 2012), and cannot recommend it highly enough.

Movement Four

[1]You can read about the official numbers in the September 2007 report by the United States Government Accountability Office titled "Number of Formally Reported Applications for Conscientious Objection Is Small Relative to the Total Size of the Armed Forces." Many organizations working in military counseling found the report's impartiality and accuracy highly suspect.

[2]Fellow Iraq Veterans Against the War member and Truth Commission on Conscience in War testifier Camilo Mejia did just that, refusing to fight a war his conscience opposed and serving nearly a year in the brig for his decision. You can learn more about his story in his book *The Road from Ar Ramadi* (New York: New Press, 2007), or in the Army-endorsed, Emmy Award–winning 2007 documentary *Soldiers of Conscience* <www.soldiers themovie.com> or <www.conscienceinwar.org>.

[3]I always found military citations of St. Francis funny, since his 1205 conversion involved his literally turning around on the road to war (in his case, the Fourth Crusade).

[4]Economics and education are intimately tied up in the politics of military recruitment; see <http://religion.blogs.cnn.com/2010/06/25/my-take-the-economic-draft>.

[5]At one point in my CO application, I was told that the constitutional right to due process did not extend to me as an active duty service member. That statement would be later refuted, quite strongly, by a number of lawyers in the Military Law Taskforce, a member organization of the National Lawyers Guild and the American Civil Liberties Union. You can read more about the task force at <http://nlgmltf.org/>.

[6]G. K. Chesterton, *What's Wrong with the World* (Charleston, S.C.: Forgotten Books, 2010), p. 39.

[7]Abraham Joshua Heschel, *I Asked for Wonder: A Spiritual Anthology* (New York: Crossroad, 1983), p. 77.

[8]This quote comes from paragraph 2309 of *The Catechism of the Catholic Church*, which articulates the just war doctrine more concretely than most traditions. The use of the term *those* seems ambiguous ("those" perhaps being the few who hold political power), but under paragraph 2239, "It is the duties of citizens to contribute *along with* the civil authorities to the good of society" (emphasis mine). Furthermore, paragraph 2242 implores the individual citizen that "refusing obedience to civil authorities, when their demands are contrary to an upright conscience, finds its justification in the distinction between serving God and serving the [country]." A more concise (and wordy) case for SCO has likely never been made.

[9]Unfortunately, the moral discernment we are called to as Christians is not recognized by the Uniform Code of Military Justice. This should be cause for significant concern within the church. For more on just war, selective objection and moral agency, see appendix A.

[10]The culture of "command discretion" currently enforced by the Uniform Code of Military Justice can be highly problematic. For example, when a service member (due to post-traumatic stress, traumatic brain injury or any number of ailments) is on psychotropic drugs, their commander can still deploy them to a combat theater against the advice of a medical professional.

[11]The passion of St. George, the patron saint of England, is recorded in *The Golden Legend*, a list of ancient saints compiled in 1260 C.E. In it we find that the dragon George slayed was actually a combination of Roman governors who demanded he worship Apollo, whom they insisted was "the savior of the world." George refused and was beheaded in 303 C.E.

[12]John Milton, *Paradise Lost* (New York: Penguin, 2001).

Movement Five

[1]Before being released on terminal leave on October 19, 2006, I was invited to participate in a rally near the Hawaii state capitol organized by The World Can't Wait, an organization with close ties to the Revolutionary Communist Party. I was allowed to be myself there, for the most part, but some of the anger and contempt that fueled a lot of peace activism (secular and religious alike) around that time certainly had an effect on me. A transcript of what I said there is on my blog at <http://feraltheology.wordpress.com/2007/10/05/no-bush-no-war-day-speech>.

[2]My reflections on that day are archived on my blog under the title "Liberty and Justice for All?" <http://feraltheology.wordpress.com/2006/10/19/liberty-justice-for-all>.

[3]Find out more about Christian Peacemaker Teams at <www.cpt.org>, where you can join a delegation, become a reservist or member, or even donate!

[4]Derek Webb, "I Don't Want to Fight," *The Ringing Bell* (INO Records, 2007). Webb's music has been incredibly helpful as I've tried to take seriously both my interest in service and my refusal to rely on violent means to achieve nonviolent ends. See particularly his album *Mockingbird* (INO Records, 2005).

[5]Five Iron Frenzy, "Every New Day," *The End Is Here* (Five Minute Walk, 2004). The block of lyrics following are from later in the same song.

[6]You can read more about the CPW at <http://christianpeacewitness.org>, or view my reading on my blog: <http://feraltheology.wordpress.com/about/cpwi>.

[7]Switchfoot, "Dare You to Move," *The Beautiful Letdown* (Columbia, 2003). Switchfoot has some really good music that spans the spectrum from grief to joy and pain to celebration. I suppose it doesn't hurt that they're from southern California; <www.switchfoot.com>.

[8]Joshua's time in Iraq overlapped with my own for a few months, and we have had the privilege of becoming friends. In his *Letters from Abu Ghraib* (Ithaca, N.Y.: Essay Press, 2008), he shares a number of emails sent in the midst of his deployment, while he worked at the infamous Abu Ghraib prison just after the scandal broke in April 2006.

[9]See <www.psalters.com> or <www.myspace.com/psalters>. I had the privilege of living with many of the Psalters during my time in Camden, which helped me see the mutuality of pacifism and the restraint of war.

[10]The Psalters, "All Who Are Weary (Missio)," *The Divine Liturgy of the Wretched Exiles* (self-produced, 2007). Also, Matthew 11:28—"Come to me, all you who are weary and burdened." All of the Psalters' stuff is identified as public domain, in keeping with their Christian anarchist beliefs (which I have great admiration for). By not copyrighting their content, it means they do not count it as "theirs" and therefore it is not something they sell. Donations help them continue doing what they do. Visit <http://psalters.org/Pages/Market/Market.html>.

[11]Jeffrey Lucy's parents, Kevin and Joyce, have spoken out about the Veterans Administration and PTSD for years. There is some question as to what Jeff experienced in war, but his story is nonetheless tragic and representative of what a number of veterans go through. <www.boston.com/yourlife/health/mental/articles/2005/03/01/jeff_lucey_returned_from_iraq_a_changed_man_then_he_killed_himself/?page=full>.

[12]I never realized that Cain's mark was actually one of protection until I reread Genesis 4 after my deployment. Before, I thought it was a mark of shame, for everyone to know that Cain had transgressed. But if you read closely, *wandering* was the curse—one that Cain claimed was "more than [he could] bear" (v. 13). God promised protection, blessing Cain with a mysterious mark, "so that no one who found him would kill him" (v. 15)—including Cain himself. Indeed, many veterans still wander, but the hope of finding home is never totally out of sight, as even Cain settled in the Land of Nod. The justice of God expressed in sentencing Cain to wandering was exceeded by the mercy made apparent in Cain's eventual settlement.

[13]I have had the pleasure of working with The Simple Way a number of times since having visited in 2006, just before my discharge. Part of my contribution has been to compile a list of resources for folks thinking through faith and service, which you can find under the "Peacemaking" section at <www.thesimpleway.org/resources/practical>.

[14]Some of those who accompanied me along the way are listed in my acknowledgments. I am eternally grateful for their friendship.

[15]In the military, we were trained to never go anywhere without a "Battle Buddy." Likewise, in Luke 10 the seventy disciples are sent out in pairs, and "the twelve apostles" are listed in pairs in Matthew 10:2-4. The only thing in all creation that God calls "not good" is to be alone (Genesis 2:18). The excruciating loneliness of the road home for veterans stands as a scathing indictment on the church's failure to be with those marked by God—not for condemnation or complacency but for protection and healing.

[16]We purposely paralleled the U.S. Oath of Enlistment, because we wanted to recycle language familiar to those serving in the Armed Forces. It also seems to provide a more gradual paradigmatic transition. That, and we aren't convinced the military is all bad. . . . You can read more about us on our website, <www.centurionsguild.org>. Sign up for email updates at <http://eepurl.com/iQ_b>.

[17]There are a couple different ways to read the story of the demon-possessed man in Mark 5:1-20, both of which are laden with the imagery of soldiers. The first, presented by New Testament scholar Richard Hays during an interview at Duke Divinity School at the After the Yellow Ribbon ceremony on Veterans Day, 2011, can be seen at <http://vimeo.com/28914544>. The second, just as thought-provoking, is in Shane Claiborne and Chris Haw, *Jesus for President* (Grand Rapids: Zondervan, 2008), pp. 114-15.

[18]Shane has included bits of the story of Rutba in his *The Irresistible Revolution: Living as an Ordinary Radical* (Grand Rapids: Zondervan, 2006); Jonathan

Wilson-Hartgrove wrote about it in detail in his *To Baghdad & Beyond: How I Got Born Again in Babylon* (Portland, Ore.: Wipf & Stock, 2005).

[19]You can read more about their inspiring stories, including becoming Hawaii's first interracial congregation in 1923, in *The Crossroads Witness* (self-published with help from University of Hawaii Press in 1988) or online at <www.churchofthecrossroadshawaii.org>.

[20]Josh Garrels, "Ulysses," *War & Love & the Sea in Between* (Small Voice, 2011). I had the opportunity to see Josh perform live at PAPA Fest 2011 in western Pennsylvania, and it was one of the best live performances ever: <www.joshgarrels.com>.

[21]My friend Jamie shot the footage for a potential documentary on our time in Rutba, check him out at <www.jamiemoffett.com>.

[22]Greg's book *The Gospel of Rutba* (Maryknoll, N.Y.: Orbis, 2012) details both the 2003 accident as well as the return in 2010 that I was privileged to have shared with the team. Find out more on Greg's website: <http://gregbarrett .org/the-gospel-of-rutba-book-film>. By the time this book went to print, I was left with significant reservations about why and how Greg grafted my story onto the (published) tale of Rutba. To detail those concerns here would be unwise, but I am nonetheless compelled to register my deep anxiety with some of his editorial and investigatory decisions surrounding the character "Logan" that he constructed. I have kept my personal reflections on Rutba somewhat limited in my book because I did not want to leave the impression that I had any idea what God was doing in and through that experience. It took me six years to reflect adequately on my military experience; any substantial interpretation of my 2010 civilian return to Iraq (from me or anyone else) risks being premature and insufficiently reflective. However, the version of Greg's book that I reviewed is both informative and inspiring, and I encourage you to pick up a copy (preferably at your local independent book seller).

[23]The psychiatrist Jonathan Shay proposes that the Sirens' song represents truth, which can be a deadly addiction for many veterans, in his *Odysseus in America: Combat Trauma and the Trials of Homecoming* (Scribner, 2003).

[24]The arched ceilings of ancient cathedrals were designed to evoke the bowels of a massive sailing vessel. Where the church congregates is thus often referred to as a "nave," from the Latin word *navis*, for a boat.

[25]Garrels, "Ulysses." See note 20 above.

[26]Rita Nakashima Brock and Gabriella Lettini, authors of *Soul Repair: Recovering from Moral Injury After War* (Boston: Beacon, 2012), organized the 2010 Truth Commission on Conscience in War, including the March 21 testimonies and the November 11 release of the commission report. Check

out <www.conscienceinwar.org>; my testimony is posted at <http://feral theology.wordpress.com/2010/03/21/tccw-testimony/>.

[27]Jericho is the site where the walls were brought down by trumpet blasts but also the setting for the parable of the Good Samaritan. Consider this: Where God's people once brought destruction we are now to bring assistance. Where once we came to bring the walls down, we have encountered the wounded traveler in need of care. Sometimes soldiers are not the heroic Samaritan; sometimes we are the voyager in distress. Having seen better days, we lie on the side of the road, marginalized and neglected, in need of compassion.

Epilogue

[1]In 2010, the rate of combat fatalities to suicides was 462:468 <www.congress .org/news/2011/01/24/more_troops_lost_to_suicide>.

[2]A CBS News report in 2007 found there to have been 6,256 suicides among veterans in 2005, and the number has increased annually since then, with some dispute as to exactly the rate of increase. To read the original article, go to <www.cbsnews.com/stories/2007/11/13/cbsnews_investigates/main 3496471.shtml>. You can also read CBS's explanation of the numbers at <www.cbsnews.com/8301-500690_162-3498625.html?tag=contentMain; contentBody>.

[3]The Psalters, "Come All You Weary (Missio)," *The Divine Liturgy of the Wretched Exiles* (self-produced, 2007).

[4]Some of this language has been recycled from my testimony at Jesus, Bombs & Ice Cream, Philadelphia, September 11, 2011. My full testimony is at <http://feraltheology.wordpress.com/video/jesus-bombs-ice-cream-testimony/>. The Simple Way has produced a beautiful study guide, available at <www.thesimpleway.org/index.php/store/product/jesus-bombs-ice-cream-dvd-resource-guide/>.

[5]This passage is drawn from the Roman Catholic Missal before the updated Third Typical Edition, released just before Advent 2011. I personally mourn the modified version, more literally reflective of the Latin ("Lord, I am not worthy to receive you under my roof, but only say the word and my soul shall be healed"); it seems to rob the verse of its literary and liturgical beauty. I fear that some might infer from the revision that "soul" is separable from self, as though my soul can be healed apart from, say, my body or my mind. I reflect on the passage (before the change) at <http://feralthe ology.wordpress.com/2011/10/17/the-war-cry>.

[6]John Paul II, *Memory and Identity: Conversations at the Dawn of a Millennium* (New York: Rizzoli, 2005).

[7]Derek Webb, "A New Law," *Mockingbird* (Integrity Media, 2008). The 2008

version has a great little audio clip at the end of Derek's thoughts on voting, which is especially relevant during any election year.

[8]Sylvia Clute does a great job of distinguishing between punitive and restorative justice in her book *Beyond Vengeance, Beyond Duality* (Charlottesville, Va.: Hampton Roads, 2010). She also blogs at <www.sylviaclute.com>.

[9]The wonderfully evocative phrase "sanctimonious trivialities" belongs to Martin Luther King Jr. He coined it in his letter from a Birmingham jail in 1963.

Permissions

✩

The following songs are quoted by permission. All rights reserved.

Derek Webb, "A New Law," *Mockingbird* (Integrity Media, 2008).

Thrice, "At the Last," *Beggars* (Vagrant, 2009).

Switchfoot, "Dare You to Move I Dare You to Move," copyright ©2000 Meadowgreen Music Company (ASCAP) Sugar Pete Songs (ASCAP) (adm. at EMICMGPublishing.com) All rights reserved. Used by permission.

Five Iron Frenzy, "Every New Day," *The End Is Here* (Five Minute Walk, 2004).

Derek Webb, "I Don't Want to Fight," *The Ringing Bell* (INO Records, 2007).

OC Supertones, "Louder Than the Mob," copyright ©1997 We Own Your Songs, Inc. (SESAC) (admin. at EMICMGPublishing.com) All rights reserved. Used by permission.

Derek Webb, "Nobody Loves Me," *The House Show* (INO Records, 2004).

Josh Garrels, "Ulysses," *War & Love & the Sea in Between* (Small Voice, 2011).

✴ ✴ ✴

The Psalters, "All Who Are Weary (Missio)," *The Divine Liturgy of the Wretched Exiles* (self-produced, 2007), is in the public domain.

✴ ✴ ✴

All effort has been made to secure permission for other quoted music.

LIKEWISE. *Go and do.*

A man comes across an ancient enemy, beaten and left for dead. He lifts the wounded man onto the back of a donkey and takes him to an inn to tend to the man's recovery. Jesus tells this story and instructs those who are listening to "go and do likewise."

Likewise books explore a compassionate, active faith lived out in real time. When we're skeptical about the status quo, Likewise books challenge us to create culture responsibly. When we're confused about who we are and what we're supposed to be doing, Likewise books help us listen for God's voice. When we're discouraged by the troubled world we've inherited, Likewise books encourage us to hold onto hope.

In this life we will face challenges that demand our response. Likewise books face those challenges with us so we can act on faith.

likewisebooks.com

31901051532465